Freestyle
Color Collage
QUILTING

Freestyle Color Collage Quilting

Landauer Publishing, www.landauerpub.com, is an imprint of Fox Chapel Publishing Company, Inc.

Project Team
Managing Editor: Gretchen Bacon
Acquisitions Editor: Amelia Johanson
Editor: Christa Oestreich
Designer: Wendy Reynolds
Proofreader & Indexer: Jean Bissell

ISBN 978-1-63981-117-5

Library of Congress Control Number: 2024945961

To learn more about the other great books from Fox Chapel Publishing, or to find a retailer near you, call toll-free 800-457-9112, send mail to
903 Square Street,
Mount Joy, PA 17552,
or visit us at www.FoxChapelPublishing.com.

We are always looking for talented authors. To submit an idea, please send a brief inquiry to acquisitions@foxchapelpublishing.com.

Note to Professional Copy Services:
The publisher grants you permission to make up to six copies of any quilt patterns in this book for any customer who purchased this book and states the copies are for personal use.

Printed in China
First printing

Freestyle
Color Collage
QUILTING

A Unique Method for Creating Bold Designs with Fabric

Carly Mul

Landauer Publishing

Freestyle collages look complicated, but the process can be broken down into easy steps. Before long, you can create stories with this new style of quiltmaking.

Contents

Introduction and Vision

Freestyle color collage is the name I have given to my technique for creating collage designs without using a pattern or a photo. You start with nothing! No pattern directions that tell you where to put a certain fabric or color value, and no shape or size to cut. Absolute creative freedom! While that may sound a little overwhelming, this book guides you to look at fabrics differently and provides much more open instructions. I hope it will teach you to "listen" to the colors, and I can assure you this sometimes means you will have to do something else than you thought.

Freestyle means natural. The flow of the colors is the way the colors want to go. Nothing stops the natural color formations in an abstract piece. For example, when you make a cat collage, your fabric needs to stay within the body contours of the cat. When you make the eyes of the cat, they need to have a certain value and a certain shape. All those restrictions disappear with freestyle color collage.

> **Trust your fabrics and trust yourself!**

There is a method to freestyle color collage, and anyone can learn it if they are willing to apply this method consistently. The colors you have on hand will determine a pattern, a path through the design. You don't know what you are going to make, which is maybe a little too open for some. Trust your fabrics and trust yourself! After all, you are using *your* fabrics and *your* colors, so the result will be a highly personal, one-of-a-kind piece that can become as big or as small as you want. It is a creative journey that is full of surprises.

Like most people who make collages, I started by making animals from patterns. It wasn't until I made my own collage, one with a lot of leaves, that my entire approach began to change. Instead of preparing one fabric at a time with adhesive web, cutting out a leaf, and positioning it on my project, I made a big sheet of fall colors by adhering different fabrics to a background without trying to create a leaf design. Using my templates, I cut multiple leaves like cutting cookies out of dough.

I loved the range of fall colors. Why did I need to cut the pieces into leaf shapes? It was obvious the colors represented the season no matter what shapes they became. That big sheet of fall colors was just as pretty, and the shapes didn't add anything to my work. I no longer needed to make an object, a form. To me, the colors were so powerful that they could tell the story, or they could be powerful in their beauty. It would be much more abstract.

My first freestyle color collage was for our home. I didn't want it to represent any specific object but knew my quilt would have to have brown, blue, and off-white: the colors of furniture, kitchen, and walls. This way, I could connect the open floorplan of our home and the colors of the kitchen and family room with my quilt. This piece has been a centerpiece in our family room ever since. You can take inspiration from anything around you and make something truly customized to your life.

I've come to love the creative process of this collage technique. The freedom of playing with fabrics can become a quilt, part of a quilt, or it can even be used as the embellishment of a jacket or other clothing! Making a freestyle color collage gives you a new way to look at colors, prints, and fabrics, which becomes helpful no matter where your quilting journey takes you. So, join me, and let's see where your journey takes you.

—Carly

There are distinct sections of color in this collage, but they still shift naturally from one to another. Go in with a plan, then "listen" to your colors.

Gallery of My Collages

This gallery of my freestyle color collages includes some of my favorites I've made through the years. Whether you want to use these as inspiration for your own work or to better understand how to create paths, these works give you a better understanding of my technique to making collages.

Organic Color Collage 1 (2022)

35" x 42" (89 x 106.7cm)
The first of my freestyle color collage quilts, which had no goal other than combining the colors brown, blue, and off-white in a quilt.

Organic Color Collage 2 (2022)

45" x 40" (114.3 x 101.6cm)
This was a request to make a freestyle color
collage for a gray room with brown furniture,
using many but not too bright colors.

The Crack (2023)

42" x 35" (106.7 x 89cm)

When I started this quilt, I had no design in mind. As it grew,
a purple line started to show up. I decided to cut my work,
following the purple line, and expand it a little. Sometimes
things are prettier because of their imperfection.

Abundance (2023)

39" x 43" (99.1 x 109.2cm)
Sample for my Houston Festival 2023 class.
I gave it the name "Abundance" because I have
so many memories of Houston Festival.

My Mother Has Alzheimer's.
These Last Five Years (2023)

43" x 36" (109.2 x 91.4cm)

This quilt is representative of the progress of Alzheimer's in my mother.
The entire quilt has been made on a muddy color that reveals itself
at the top, as does the disease. First there are just a few spots, and as
the disease progressed, they became bigger and more numerous.

In Paradiso (2024)

45" x 29" (114.3 x 73.6cm)
Dealing with my mother's terminal illness, I made this quilt
during the last weeks of her life. The colors are inspired
by Italian Renaissance frescoes we saw together so often.

Neighborhoods (2024)

35½" x 39" (90.2 x 99.1cm)

This quilt is inspired by the colors of Dutch architecture. The color combinations used on buildings and streets are not seen anywhere else. The very dark, almost black, green is called "canal green" and is used on window frames and doors.

Growing Color (2024)

45½" x 32" (115.6 x 81.3cm)

A quilted encouragement to look for little things that bring us joy, even when not perfect. Here, my freestyle color collage technique has been used for the background.

Gene Pool (2024)

38" x 37" (96.5 x 94cm)
My most recent collage in shades of blues. When I think "blue," my
family comes to mind. Not only do we all love this color, but we
also share many of the same values despite being so different.

Bouquet (2024)

43½" x 45" (96.5 x 94cm)

I was inspired by local vineyards to create a quilt
where the colors of growing vines give a visual
to the different blends and aromas we taste.

Supplies and Notions

Fabric collage is making quilts with lots of little pieces of fabric. The goal is to put these fabrics together in such a way to form a pleasing result. Despite my quilts developing organically, I still follow a method, which requires certain tools and materials for every project.

Fabric

Any 100% cotton can be used for collage. I really would stay away from noncotton fabrics, especially in the beginning. Different materials create different heights and effects, and with that, you could get some fabrics sticking or textural effects that you hadn't intended. I cover Fabric Categories in-depth starting on page 25, but in general, any 100% cotton fabric will suit my method.

If you're committing to this style of quilting, forget about throwing any fabric away! Even the tiniest scraps can find a place in your freestyle color collage, which I also like to call organic color collage. And yes, "ugly" fabrics are just as valuable as your favorite ones. You can mix batiks with super modern or reproduction fabrics. Blenders, plaids, flowers, novelty,

digitally printed fabrics: all these cotton fabrics have color and thus can play a role in the process.

HOW IMPORTANT IS A STASH?

It would be difficult to make a freestyle color collage without a fabric stash because achieving the look we

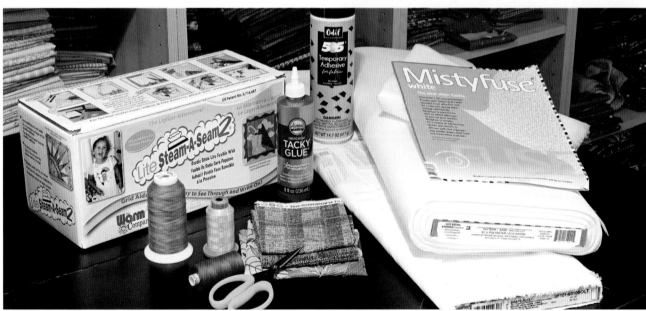

The main materials you need for collage are ways to adhere fabric to a base, such as fusible, glue, and thread.

want requires a tremendous amount of fabric. When you want to buy fabric for a collage quilt, look for the smallest amounts you can get. In most stores, this is a fat quarter; unfortunately, a fat quarter is a giant in collage minds. You can look at charm packages, but the disadvantage is they are prepackaged, so you won't know exactly which prints or colors are included—although, if you can find the collection online, the color array is usually pictured. In addition, precut fabrics are often *too* coordinated. You may lose that organic sensibility when you put your faith in a preselected collection.

My collage quilts use small pieces, anywhere between ½" and 4" (1.3 and 10.2cm), and I seldom use the same fabric twice in one quilt. That means a tremendous amount of fabric is needed. My quilts, which are typically around 42" (106.7cm), include anywhere from 600–700 pieces of fabric in them. I have tried several times to count them but lost track. Some pieces are bigger than 4" (10.2cm), but that is rare. Even in that case, it could be a piece 6" (15.2cm) tall but then as narrow as ½" (1.3cm). Most pieces are between 1" and 3" (2.5 and 7.6cm).

When working with collage, you will appreciate a big stash of fabrics. Even better: a big stash of scraps. Whatever anyone else is throwing away is a treasure for you! You can also ask your quilting friends if you may have a little bit of their fabrics. In my experience, most people are happy to help you out. They are often intrigued by what you can do with so many little pieces.

My ideal way of organization is sorting by color; the top shelves are light, and the fabrics become darker moving down.

Collage uses a lot of colors and prints, so you want a wide variety in your stash.

I've built up a large collection after running a fabric store. No matter the size of your fabric stash, sorting by color is an easy way to stay organized.

When a fabric is too small to fold neatly, it goes in a tray.

HOW I ORGANIZE MY FABRICS

I have many shelves with fabrics (19 years of owning a fabric store has given me a treasure trove of smaller cuts, and yet I still buy *a lot* of fabric). Most are a ½ yard (45.7cm) maximum. I fold all these fabrics from selvage to selvage for storage. This way, they end up all having the same width on my shelves.

I stack most of my cotton prints by color; larger folds together, and fat quarters or smaller folds together. I also have a stack of multicolored fabrics organized by whatever color is the most dominant (usually the background color). When fabric pieces are too small to fold neatly, they go in trays, which are stacked by color under my worktable.

I say "most of my cotton prints" because I have separate shelving for specific brands, novelty prints, Australian, batiks, and metallics. Within those, I also have separate trays or bins with scraps. You'll be surprised at how much fabric you will accumulate once you decide to hang on to all your bits and scraps. That's why it's important to organize by color for this technique.

STORAGE FOR SMALL SPACES

Space and quilting are in a difficult relationship. Nobody ever has enough space for storage or for their workspace. We all have to do with whatever we have, and we all are always looking for ways to improve. It is all about the accessibility of fabrics: how can I find what I need?

Each person starts with nothing. In my experience, quilters upgrade from plastic bags, nicer plastic bags, bins, to fancier bins. It is the journey of the quilter and highly personal. The more you accumulate, the more storage comes in the picture. There is no one right way of storage. So whether you are using small plastic drawers on a desk, bins under your bed, or shelves on a wall, any option that works for you is correct.

Different quilting techniques require different sorting systems. For freestyle collage, I sort on colors. Someone who makes a lot of scrappy quilts may sort their fabrics by size or shape. If tight on space, many quilters cut their leftovers right away in the sizes of their choice. Learn more about this in the section on Preparing Fabrics (page 51). This way, you aren't keeping stacks of fabric but the small pieces you already plan on using.

Foundation

This thin paper works as the foundation of your collage. You will apply your fabric pieces directly to the material, and it will serve as the quilt top when complete. For my collage technique, I find Pattern Ease to be invaluable. It comes on a bolt that is 46" (116.8cm) wide, and you can usually purchase it by the yard.

While you can work directly on a background fabric, Pattern Ease is a much more economical choice. It gives you the flexibility to decide what you want to do with your collage at a later point. Once it's done, you can lift your work and put it on a background fabric or straight on the batting. The foundation stays in your quilt, which is not a problem, as most organic color collage quilts are intended to be wall hangings. It also adds a little bit of stiffening, which is nice because it makes the quilt hang straighter.

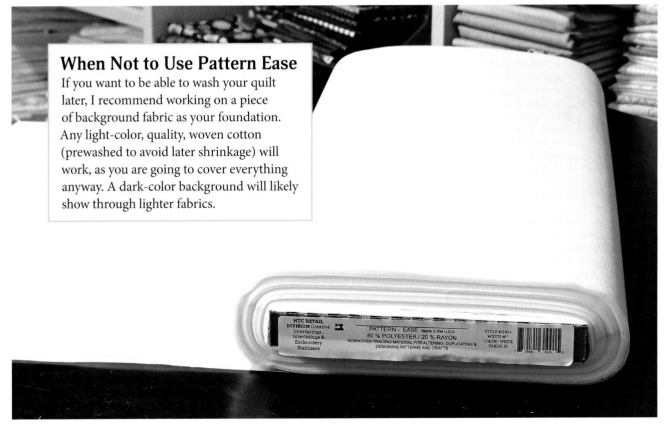

When Not to Use Pattern Ease

If you want to be able to wash your quilt later, I recommend working on a piece of background fabric as your foundation. Any light-color, quality, woven cotton (prewashed to avoid later shrinkage) will work, as you are going to cover everything anyway. A dark-color background will likely show through lighter fabrics.

Pattern Ease makes for a good collage base that will also add structure to the finished piece.

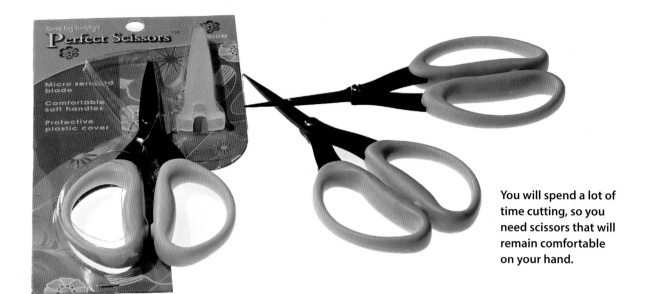

You will spend a lot of time cutting, so you need scissors that will remain comfortable on your hand.

Scissors

You need a pair of good scissors that make cutting comfortable on your hand. I strongly recommend Karen Kay Buckley's Perfect Scissors™, the medium-size (blue) ones. You'll find that many collage authors and teachers use these particular scissors because they are designed to be comfortable when held, and the serrated edges make cutting fabric easier. Of course, you may prefer a different brand, but the key is a quality scissor with a good, sharp blade.

Fusible Web

Fusible webbing is a glue that attaches to a fabric background. This is especially useful for appliqué, and easier than traditional needle turn, because you can trace the shape on paper first and then iron it down. Fusibles come in different thicknesses, stiffness results, and with or without paper to draw a shape on first.

The market is gigantic and new fusibles are coming out all the time. That may be confusing to new quilters, but with fusibles, the first question to ask is: why do I

Choose a fusible that is repositionable, which allows for a natural collage process.

Batting adds warmth and loft to your quilted piece.

want to use a fusible? Second: what does it need to do for me? That will steer you into a direction.

To replicate my freestyle collage technique, you need a fusible webbing that is repositionable. Currently, Lite Steam-A-Seam 2 (LSAS2) is the only product that works with my collage technique. This fusible interfacing not only attaches your fabrics well to the foundation, but it also adheres to the background before ironing it down. Best of all—it is moveable. LSAS2 essentially makes your fabric piece into a sticker.

As long as you don't iron down a piece of fabric prepared with LSAS2, it can be moved around without losing any of its future permanent bonding. You can pick it up and place it somewhere else, which is extremely important when you aren't yet sure where a fabric is going to end up. Once you take full advantage of LSAS2, your work will grow to a much more creative level.

LSAS2 is available in several widths: ¼", 2½", 9", 12", 18", and 24" (0.6, 6.4, 22.9, 30.5, 45.7, and 61cm). None of the narrow widths (9" [22.9cm] or below) work very well for freestyle color collage. You can use them, but you're going to be making a lot more work for yourself. What you need is yardage, and for that, look for LSAS2 in 3 yard (2.7m) rolls, which can be purchased either 18" or 24" (45.7 or 61cm) wide. If you're really committing to freestyle color collage, you can even find 40 yard (36.6m) rolls; I use this, preferring the 12" (30.5cm) width. I keep it next to my ironing board, and whenever I have a few fabrics to prepare, I just roll out the amount I need and get to work. **Note:** There is also a regular version of this fusible, but I find it has more glue on it than necessary, so I prefer the Lite version.

Batting

Batting is available as two-sided fusible, one-sided fusible, or nonfusible batting. You can get battings made from cotton, wool, silk, bamboo, poly, and mixed materials. For projects like this, I prefer to work with one-sided fusible batting. It's important to me that the batting is thin. My pieces are usually turned into wall hangings, which means a firmer batting is helpful. Any batting that shows stitching nicely will do. I also prefer fusible batting, as it eliminates the process of basting.

It is all very much a matter of personal preference. Your work will not get washed later, so many of the differences between all the different kinds of battings disappear a little. You don't see the benefits of one option above another, and the choice of your batting doesn't change much when the quilt is not getting washed.

If you have nonfusible batting lying around, you can use that without a problem. The world of batting has many options, and I haven't found any double-sided fusible batting that is thin enough for my taste. They all have too much loft.

A collage with a lot of color will require many thread colors to match and enhance the piece.

Stabilizer adds structure to a wall hanging or other quilted project.

Thread

Collecting threads is just as much fun as collecting fabrics! I use threads to blend the fabrics even better. Any thread that is 12–60 wt. is fine. For collage, it can be cotton, poly, or rayon thread. Here, too, it is all about color. Take advantage of the small boxes of various colors that are available for quilters. You won't need big spools, as you are not sewing large areas in the same color; instead, you will switch threads often. I try to use only Superior Threads™ Bottom Line in my bobbin. This thread is 60 wt. and can handle most top threads.

Optional Supplies

- **Fusible stabilizer** adds body to your work and makes the collage hang better. I recommend Shape-Flex®, which comes in two widths, 20" and 60" (50.8 and 152.4cm). It is nice to have a width that covers your entire work without any seams, so for any collage wider than 20" (50.8cm), the

60" (152.4cm) width is the size of choice. Shape-Flex is available in two colors, white and black. Try to get the one that works best with your fabrics. Usually this is the white, unless your work is much darker.

- **Fabric glue** can create a temporary hold before stitching pieces of fabric together. It will wash out without ruining your piece. In this book, it is used to make the "wrap-and-glue" binding (page 86). You won't need this product otherwise for your collage. Aleene's Original Tacky Glue is the brand I prefer.

- **Webbing and adhesive sprays** can be used to baste your quilt. You will most likely be laying your collage onto backing and batting for the quilting process (see page 81), and an adhesive spray between the layers will help keep your layers from moving during the stitching process. I have used both Mistyfuse® webbing and Odif 505 Temporary Fabric Adhesive spray.

Fabric Categories

Freestyle color collage is fabric driven. That's the good news. The not-so-good news is that choosing fabrics seems to be the most difficult part for many of my students. In this chapter, I explain in detail (with loads of examples graciously provided by fabric manufacturers) how to go about selecting each print or color for your project.

No matter what style quilter you are, no matter what palette of colors you have in your stash, the same rules will apply for my technique. You will quickly find that the fabrics you preferred for a traditionally pieced quilt project may not necessarily be the fabrics you'll need for your collage. There is no difference between batiks or regular cottons, reproduction fabrics or modern, extra-wide fabrics or regular width. Every piece of fabric has a color, and that's all that matters.

To help you get a better grasp on using fabric in organic color collage, I divide fabrics into five main categories: Leaders, Followers, Connectors, Kisses, and Solids. You'll see several examples of each and learn how some fabrics can be both. By the time we are done, you will be able to look at your stash or walk into a store and immediately recognize which fabrics are which, and why they may or may not be good collage fabrics.

Most people (even store owners) gravitate to certain fabrics—similar prints, similar colorways, even the same manufacturers—but in freestyle color collage, we learn to appreciate fabrics that are a little outside a personal box. I don't want to change anyone's love for a certain style of fabric! I love Kaffe Fassett, and I use his prints all the time in my work. I just want you to be open to everything that can expand your creativity.

Everything you learn about selecting fabrics will come together as you begin to place your pieces on your background. When I talk about fabric here, I do allude to placement, for example, how a Follower might pair with a Leader. This will become clearer when we start to talk about lines and pathways in Creating a Path (page 38).

These trays are stacked by color under my worktable.

Leaders

A Leader is a fabric that has a certain shape in its design, ready to cut out. For instance, a flower, star, circle, or paisley. Subtle shapes, such as the tail of an animal or a cup of tea, also have an outspoken design that you can cut out. To be a Leader, this fabric design has to be big enough to get noticed. In general, pieces need to be at least 1" (2.5cm) in diameter, unless it is a long narrow piece like a branch.

A Leader can have one or multiple colors. Leaders are the main fabrics in your collage, meant to grab your attention, and they lead the way the eye will go. Leaders can also be called the focus fabrics or main fabrics. Flowers and other elements of nature often make good Leaders because they are typically printed large. They can be found with modern and traditional companies alike. Leaders are not so hard to find. You will develop an eye for it. The hardest part of Leaders is to find some in the colors of your choice.

Most Leaders don't come in full collections but there are some wonderful exceptions. The designs of Kaffe Fassett (and the Kaffe Fassett Collective) very often make excellent Leaders. Kaffe is known for his bright colors, but a closer look will show you excellent darks and pastels as well. Every quilt I made has many Kaffe prints in it. You can start with his fabrics, such as his newest collections, to guarantee a good Leader.

Deco by Kaffe Fassett for FreeSpirit Fabrics has several colors, and they are not overly bright. Actually, his use of mid browns is very new!

Lotus Leaf by Kaffe Fassett for FreeSpirit Fabrics comes in many colors, and each fabric gives multiple options for Leaders.

Good finds are fabrics that offer multiple Leaders like Goodness Gracious! Embrace from Windham Fabrics.

There are some very packed Leaders in Goodness Gracious! Back in the Day from Windham Fabrics.

With all the flowers being about 2" (5.1cm) wide, Copacetic Main from Riley Blake Designs offers you multiple Leaders.

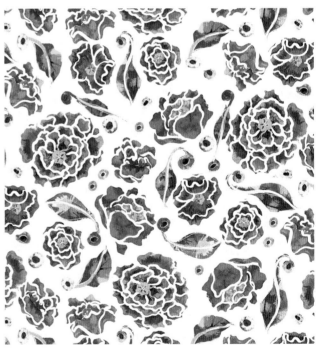

Tiny Wonders by KG Art Studio for P&B Textiles is a more abstract Leader.

When you cut the large leaves in Botanical Beauties by Laundry Basket Quilts for Andover Fabrics, you can see the unusual color combinations.

In Koi Pond from P&B Textiles, these leaves make great Leaders.

Because Begins with Mum Calendula from Benartex is in one color, I would use only one flower for one project. It's a consideration that is up to you on how to use.

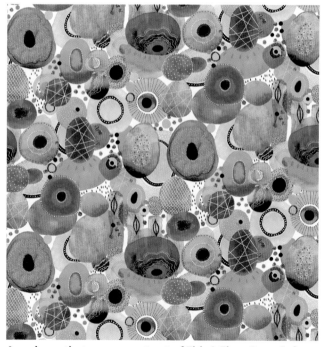

Any shape that you can cut out of Ebb & Flow Genesis from Windham Fabrics is fairly large and can be considered a Leader.

The main fabric of Indigo Song from P&B Textiles has multiple Leaders in the pink, yellow, and blue flowers. The little birds can make a cute little accent at the end.

The Afternoon Tea panel of Teacup from Windham Fabrics has some flowers, a bowl, and the spout of a teapot to make into a Leader. It is all about the cutline a design provides!

Kindred Blush from Moda can be used for many Leaders but also has plenty of fabric to be used as a Solid.

Kisses

Kisses are fabrics that have a certain shape that you can cut out, but they are too little to be called a Leader. Kisses are around ½"–1" (1.3–2.5cm). They are important because they add whimsy to your work and soften the look. Most of the time, Kisses have multiple colors, but they can be one color as well.

My quilts have many parts that came from novelty scraps. By taking a fresh eye to the prints and being creative with which parts can be cut out, you can find Kisses and Leaders where you might not expect! Turn the shape around and nobody will ever see the original use!

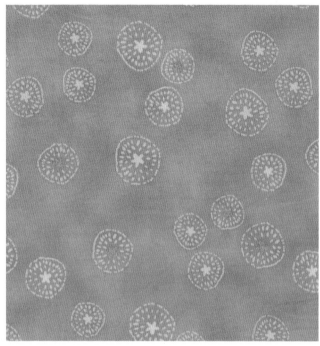

Flirtation Blooming by Moda is a very organic-looking Kiss.

Day of the Dead Skull Folklore from Timeless Treasures can be fussy cut to create Kisses in the eyes, teeth, etc.

Pickleball Paddles and Balls from Northcott gives Kisses in its little pickleballs!

Followers or Blenders

Followers are fabrics that have very little character themselves, usually called "blenders": tonal fabrics with a tiny, random design in it. There are no shapes in the print that will tell you how to cut. Followers have only one color, or maybe one color with a little bit of white or beige. A Follower is a fabric that follows a Leader. It makes a Leader stronger by letting it shine more or making its impact bigger.

Most people have lots of scrappy blenders in their stash. Good! You will need many, even though most students don't recognize them in my quilts right away. That's why these fabrics are Followers; the attention goes to a Leader. On the other hand, if you put Leaders closely together, they are fighting to become the strongest, and the work will look messy. Followers are important to have, as they space out the Leaders.

Followers are the easiest fabrics to find. It's just a matter of finding the right shade, but with so many options, that is not such a challenge. The most obvious examples are big lines of basics that every company makes. The advantage? The prints are available in many colors, and that helps in finding a match. Followers can also often be found as part of a collection. There, it supports the main fabric, usually as sashing or a background.

Followers can be fabrics on their own, but they can also be found in the spacing of Leader designs. Look at the detail of a fabric, such as dots between flowers. The Leader is obvious on a print, but it could very well be that there is a Follower that you can use.

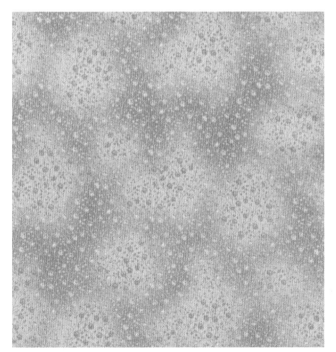

Use only the light blue or medium blue areas of Fusions® from Robert Kaufman Fabrics for perfect Followers.

Dimples from Andover Fabrics make a great textured Follower.

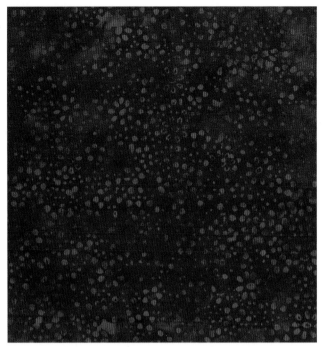

Daisy Dots from Windham Fabrics could be a Leader, but cut it in a random shape, and it turns into a Follower.

The lines on Grass Roots from P&B Textiles do not need to be cutting lines. It can be cut in any shape.

The textural red in Pepita by Stephanie Brandenburg for Northcott is a clear Follower that will support a Leader well.

Grunge fabrics from Moda have become a quilting staple. A grunge that has one color is a Follower, but if it has multiple colors, it is a Connector.

Connectors

Connectors are fabrics that have two or more colors in them but no obvious design to cut out. Think multicolored blenders with dots, hearts, or stripes. Connectors make a bridge. They help you go from one main color to the other main color, from Leader to Leader. Connectors are a little bit more interesting than Followers because they have at least two or more colors. However, they lack a shape to cut out.

Connectors are harder to find because you need to have a Connector that has the exact two colors of the Leaders you've chosen. A Connector needs to go well with two Leaders, sometimes more, to make that connection work.

Sometimes a print can open your mind. You may not have had the plan to move your collage toward fuchsia, for example, then suddenly you've bumped into a print that allows for that possibility. Listen to your fabric! You could easily ignore the fuchsia and follow another color in the print. These options come in handy if you have a Leader but have no idea where to go to next. The Connector opens the way to different color families.

Softer, more muted color Connectors are much harder to find than brights. The reason for this? Connectors are part of a collection, and they are supportive fabrics for the main print. Fabric companies make many more bright and clear colors as the main fabric. It's simply a matter of what would sell better, and in general, brighter colors sell better than muted.

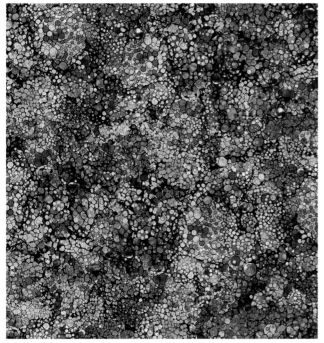

Bliss Basics from Northcott is a collection in many colors, which could connect different colors depending on which you choose.

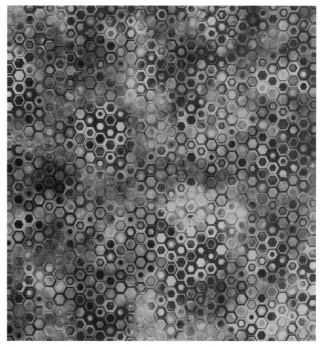

This particular colorway of Phantasma from Robert Kaufman Fabrics will connect azure with fuchsia.

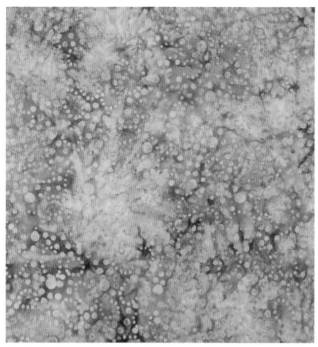

The subtle shading of Batiks Bayou Expressions Marina Batiks from Riley Blake Designs makes a great bridge between a blue and a green Leader.

Scrawl Punc. from Andover Fabrics is a sample of a contemporary print that connects two different greens.

Bali Calypso Forget Me Not from Benartex opens up a connection to four colors.

The little flowers in Fragrant Fen Florescence from FreeSpirit Fabrics can bridge toward orange, blue, peach, or darker green.

Utopia Small Metallic Paint Splatters from Timeless Treasures Fabrics can connect the background color to any of the colors in the splatter.

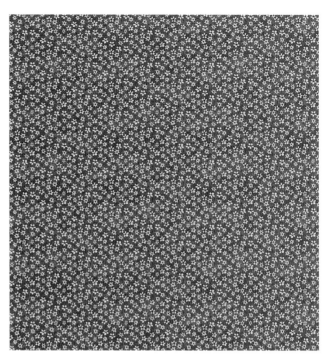

Berry Pickers from Northcott can connect the background color to any of the four other colors in the flowers.

Fluidity from Northcott can connect purple, blue, and green because it is a much more abstract print.

Live Out Loud Dream Big from FreeSpirit Fabrics has unusual color combinations, which makes it unique. To connect, you need to know which colors you are looking for.

Solids

Solids are fabrics that have no design. By definition, a Solid is always one color. You can use Solids within your organic collage, but the lack of design will make them stand out in the middle of all the other fabrics. I use Solids sparingly. In "The Crack" (page 10), I used Solids in the border and there they have a function: creating contrast. "Growing Color" (page 15) is a good example of how Solids are also very nice to use on top of your collage as an appliqué.

Category Breakers

Even though I've established five fabric categories, as most fabrics do meet the criteria for at least one of the five, I must admit that not every fabric is so clear. In many cases, it depends on how you cut the fabric.

Radiance from Windham Fabrics is an excellent large circle print, but if you don't cut out the circle, it becomes a Follower.

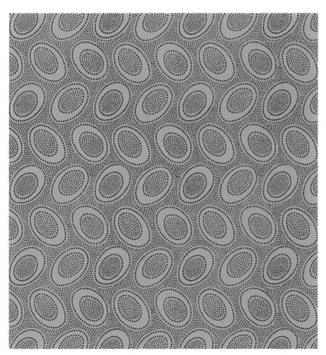

Aboriginal Dots by Kaffe Fassett is too big for a Kiss, but it's not really a Leader either. I cut out the shape but use it as a Follower.

Paper Trees Leaf Pile by Sue Penn from FreeSpirit Fabrics can be considered a Leader but could also work as a Connector.

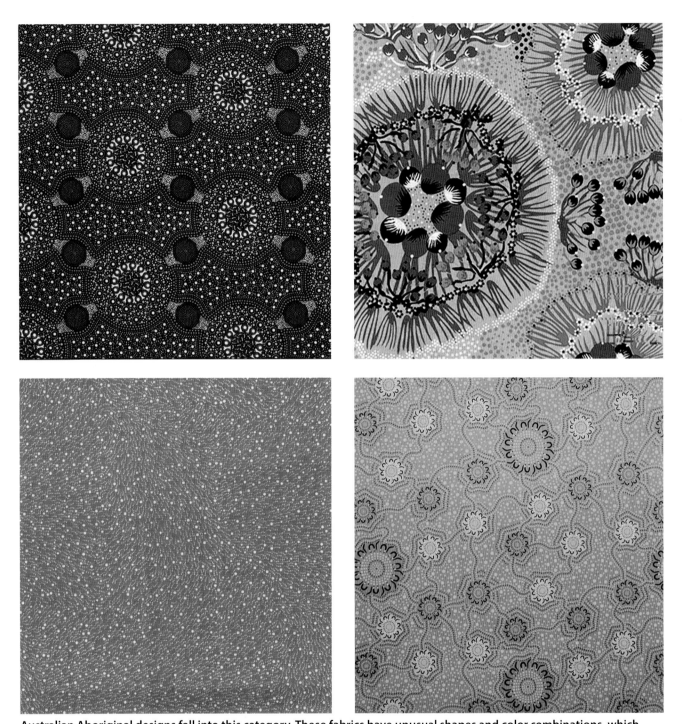

Australian Aboriginal designs fall into this category. These fabrics have unusual shapes and color combinations, which make them an excellent resource for freestyle color collage. It's easy to see Leaders, Followers, Connectors, and Kisses in any of them.

Creating a Path

When little toddlers learn about different kinds of animals, they're taught to recognize the features of the animals. Then they can label the animal as a giraffe, a cat, or a spider, to name three examples. Adults do this too. We have so much experience in seeing animals that this scanning and labeling happens in milliseconds, and we hardly have to look. A little child checks the image from top to bottom. Their eyes and brains travel the road from top to bottom, from the head to the tail. The eyes move and follow the features. A long neck? Giraffe!

In a freestyle color collage, your eyes follow the same process of scanning and moving the eyes around

Toddlers learn to recognize the features of an animal based on its shape.

the image, but the result is not a giraffe or bird, it is abstract. These collages are about looking and finding enjoyment in that process of scanning. The colors may evoke a feeling in you: pleasure or surprise, sadness or joy, or even nostalgia. Maybe the image does look like something you recognize, or it reminds you of something. Maybe it doesn't remind you of anything at all, but it is just fascinating to see. This is what is magical about my organic approach!

One of the comments I hear about my quilts quite often is that there is so much to see, and it changes all the time. Movement. It is unknown territory for the viewer and he or she is challenged to look like a little child might. What do you see? It's ever changing, depending on who is looking.

That road your eyes travel from one point to another is a path or pathway. It can be from left to right, from right to left, on a diagonal, or any direction. It can make curves. The path takes your eyes in a certain direction. It moves you from one spot to the other, like a river. It starts at point A and ends at point B. It can be tiny short or endlessly long, and in freestyle color collage those pathways are created by color.

Color

When I talk about color, I talk about the flow. The road the colors take you from one spot to the other in a smooth and consistent manner—a natural path. It feels like it must go a certain way, and your eyes almost follow effortlessly from one transition to the next.

The flow of color is the result of the connection between each tiny little element of color. Every little spot has its place in the bigger picture. The flow can be described as the smooth movement of lots of little paths or of one big path. It is a matter of how detailed you want to look. How much do you zoom in? For instance: You decide the quilt is going from yellow to orange to red. Or you can have the quilt go from lemon to sunshine, from melon to tangerine, from rose to burgundy. These are different levels of detail in

Your eye will likely be drawn to a Leader first, then travel around this piece following "paths" of color, pattern, or interest.

There are some dramatic changes of color in this work in progress, but smaller color palettes are just as beautiful.

The first collage finished by one of my students, Anne Mullins, shows an amazing eye for color despite her being new to collage.

It's easiest to start making paths in a straight line. When feeling confident with the process, you can work up to more complex designs.

describing and looking. What they have in common is the movement of color. Flow is a change, a movement in connections. These connections are like relationships and, as we all know, relationships can change.

Plenty of books have been written about the theory of color and the different kinds of flows. I will keep it a little bit more pragmatic and teach you how you can make a smooth and even color path with your quilting fabric by looking at what you have. The fabric guides you but can only do this as far as you can see it. There is an interaction between you and your fabric—you work together. In my method, I can help you create smooth transitions. My approach even works for those who feel they don't have an eye for color or don't consider themselves creative.

Anyone can learn and follow my directions. I find no bigger reward than when a student is pleasantly surprised by what they have made. It's a wonderful and encouraging moment.

Path or pathway is a word that shows you movement. It is open ended; not very strict, yet creative. Creating a path is the goal when we work with fabrics in organic color collage. To understand this process, I first have to show you some possible paths. In the beginning, these paths will be more like a line. It is my experience that some firmer guidelines in the beginning help you understand the process better. When you know how to make a line by going from point A to point B and feel comfortable doing this, you will dare to expand your pathways. To me, the word *line* and *path* express some kind of thought process, but line is a little more analytical and path a little broader and more creative. I will use both terms.

How Do We Create a Path?

The simplest line is going from dark to light or from light to dark. Let's say you want to go from dark blue to light blue. You can take any color blue and put the fabric in color order, going dark to light. This line can go all the way to white. It can have a length of two colors (dark and light blue), three colors (dark, medium, and light), or it can become a long, even endless, line with numerous shades and values of blue if you have that many fabrics.

While the eye will obviously follow the blues when arranged in a straight line, they still travel the same

Blue swatches arranged in a straight line.

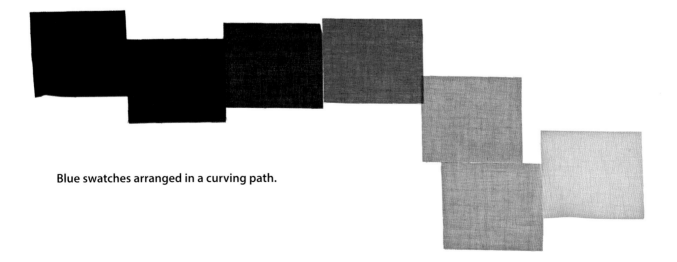

Blue swatches arranged in a curving path.

path when arranged in new layout. In the curving path, for example, doesn't your gaze dip down to the blue-gray square despite the faster route being from sky blue to gray? Because there is an obvious path, even when made by a small link, your eye will naturally trace the colors in order.

As long as the order of the colors is correct, a path will be formed. A gradient or ombre fabric does this well. What could break this line? Adding another color anywhere will break it up. It is a stranger. Even putting a lighter shade in the wrong spot can achieve the same effect.

We all know there are different kinds of blues: some are a little more purple, some are a little greener, some are brighter, and some are duller. This is not a book about color theory, and you don't have to know anything about color theory to make freestyle color collage quilts. What you do need are eyes that can see the difference between these different blues (and other colors). Sometimes, it is not so easy to see which color is darker than another color, but our phones are amazing tools. You can take a picture and use a gray filter, which will show you if all the colors are in the right order.

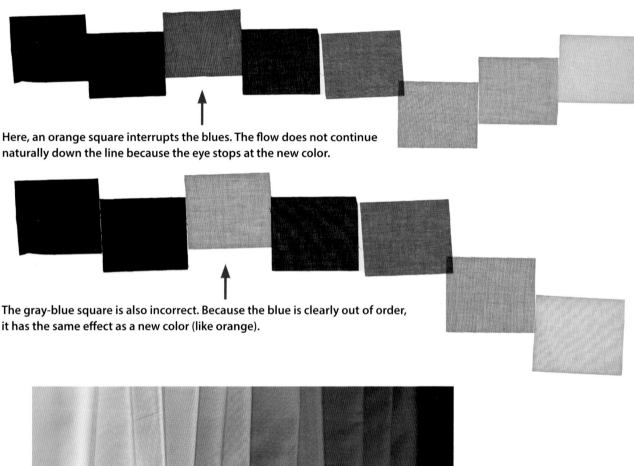

Here, an orange square interrupts the blues. The flow does not continue naturally down the line because the eye stops at the new color.

The gray-blue square is also incorrect. Because the blue is clearly out of order, it has the same effect as a new color (like orange).

A proper gradient of blues may not be obvious until you make the image grayscale.

Practice Reading Your Fabrics

Let's run through a little lesson on when and how to read fabrics for placement using a selection of blues.

Step 1: Here we have an assortment of blues from a similar color family. At first it looks a bit messy. But examine closer: some are light blue, others are more gray blue, still others are aqua blue. They can take us in different directions.

Step 2: Instead of putting all these fabrics together in one blue group, going from dark to light, it would be much better to split the blues into little piles of similar colors. Don't think Leaders, Followers, Connectors, or Kisses just yet. Only look at the color, and group similar colors together. What you name your groups isn't important, just look for a way to divide the original pile into pleasant-looking combinations that coordinate more closely. This isn't an exact science.

On page 44, see how I ended up with six piles, because that was the natural division, the way my eyes saw it. You might find that five piles work for your project, or perhaps seven. If you don't like a piece with an existing group, you simply start another "pile." This step is about grouping your pieces so that they are pleasing to you, the artist, and your eyes. I tend to be quite particular here, because the more cohesive a grouping is, the prettier the paths will become.

Step 3: In the six piles, I ended up with three larger groups at the bottom and three smaller groups at the top. Important: Treat all these piles as if they are

The more fabrics you have, the more variations in color you will see.

Miscellaneous

Dark Blue

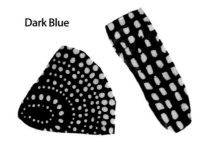

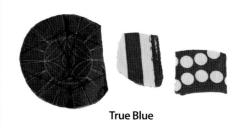

True Blue

Aqua Blue

Sky Blue

Gray Blue

The pieces are sorted into six groups, depending on the colors I believe are the most dominant.

completely different colors; the only way to put them together later is applying the rules for moving to a completely different color to connect them. When a group is as small as the top three groups, it means that I probably won't use these in my project—at least not yet. Sometimes you will find more blues later and the piles can grow and become useful.

Step 4: It's not until we group our fabrics that we can identify within each group the possible Leader and its Followers and Connectors. It could very well be that your group has no Leader, which means you can't use that group quite yet, as every pathway should start with a Leader. Set that group aside until you create an opening for it to fit into your collage (which may or may not happen).

It could be that you have no Followers or Connectors in your groupings; it's just a group of potential Leaders. If there are two really strong Leaders you want to use in your piece, go back to your stash; you're on the hunt for additional blues that will take you from one Leader to the other. As you'll learn later, we generally avoid placing two Leaders next to each other. Treat these groups as if they are individual colors. Aqua blue can only stay next to gray blue if a Connector can be found to link the groups.

In my quilt "Organic Color Collage 2" (page 9), you can clearly see how I divided the different teals.

With our fabrics roughly organized, we are ready to lay down our first path, but the path you intended to travel may not take you where you thought it might lead. It's not unlike life in this way, and that's the joy of this technique.

Moving to a Completely Different Color

Let's say you don't want to go from dark to light, but instead, you want to go from one color to a completely different color. It's a little more complex. How do you do this?

Example 1: Purple to Green

The following sample goes from purple to green: purple on the left, green on the right. The striped fabric in the middle is the perfect middle, as it is exactly half purple and half green. This fabric is extremely important. Without it, the purple and green are strangers to each other. The stripes give them a relationship, connection, or link. Together, they are a path, starting at purple and ending at green.

The path can be expanded a little bit more: purple, mainly purple with some green, mainly purple with more green, equal amount of purple and green, mainly green with some purple, mainly green with a tiny bit of purple, green. The fabrics that have more purple than green (over 50 percent purple) should stay closer to the

A path from purple to green with a perfect Connector in the middle.

   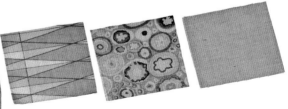

Expand the path with fabrics that have different amounts of purple and green.

purple. Usually, it is easy to identify the fabric with the most purple in it; this is something you don't have to measure. You can see it. If you are in doubt, the fabric choices are probably about even, and it doesn't matter what order they are in. We are not doing real math.

The image on the bottom of this page shows that I didn't have a green fabric with just purple in my stash. The fabric has other colors as well, but it still reads mostly green. For the green-purple line, I am ignoring these other colors. The line is working, because the fabric has percentages of both green and purple, and all these greens and purples are dominant colors.

What is important to see is that every fabric on this path has purple or green, which is what all these fabrics have in common. Their relationship is about purple and green. Some have more purple, some have more green, but the line can only be made by fabrics that have either or both of those colors as the main color. Every other color would break the line and be a stranger. Fabrics that have other colors than purple and green are fine as long as the color purple and green are dominant.

This line can expand in many directions depending on the availability of purple and green in your stash. Maybe you have a lot of purple fabrics but not so many purples with greens? No problem. The purple section would be bigger, and that is okay, because purple is probably one of your favorite colors to work with. Let those purples shine!

USING A THIRD COLOR

Let's say you still want to go from purple to green, but you have no purple-and-green fabric in your stash. You need to have good reasons to want to do this, but you can! This requires the help of another color that can make the connections and create a line with three main colors in it: purple, green, and X. X can be any color that connects them. No color wheel knowledge

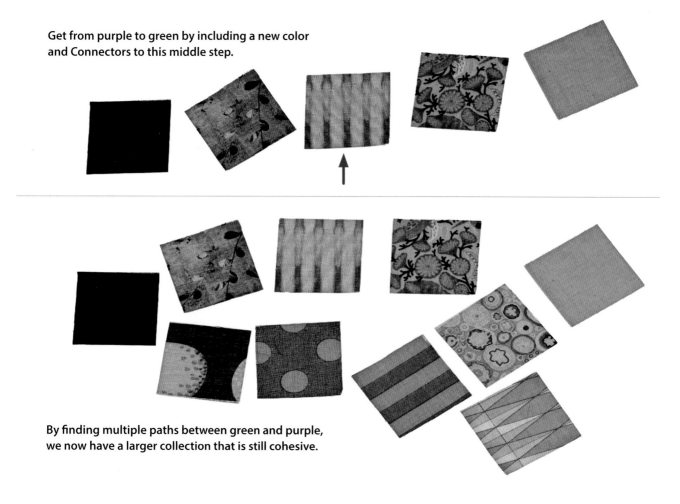

Get from purple to green by including a new color and Connectors to this middle step.

By finding multiple paths between green and purple, we now have a larger collection that is still cohesive.

is necessary. Fabric designers have the work done for you by creating beautiful color combinations in their collections, so search your stash and look for a fabric that has some purple with another color (your X) and another fabric that is green with that same X color.

In my stash, I found these teals for fabric X. Teal is my connection, so I have one purple with teal, one green with teal, and even a good teal for in the middle! When I want to go from purple to green, I can now get there indirectly. The mostly purple with teal needs to stay closer to the purple, the stripes can be in the middle, and the green-with-teal print is the one closer to green.

When I put these teals together with the previous expanded purple-green line, you can see that I have now found two ways to get from one endpoint to another. Because both are perfect paths coming from the same start and ending at the same point, there is harmony. Harmony is a loaded word in color theory. Without knowing anything about the color wheel, let's say: They look good together. This is much more practical, and this book is about looking.

In a way, the purple-to-green line is determined by the fabric that I found for the middle. This middle can be a purple-green stripe or a teal. All the fabrics you can use on the line are determined by the middle fabric. I call that the reference point (RP) of the line. The RP tells you which fabric needs to be closer to the purple or closer to the green. If a fabric is greener than the reference point, it should go between the RP and green. If the fabric is more purple than the reference point, the fabric goes in between purple and RP. Even though you have no pattern, these rules leave you little choice, and it is pretty clear where the next fabric needs to go.

EXPANDING ON THE PATH

After the teals, I found a fabric that is mostly green with teal, fuchsia, and black in it. Where can it go? If I don't want to break my lines, this fabric must be placed in between the teal and green. As this particular fabric has some fuchsia and black in it, I can make the line longer and longer. I started with purple and green, but now I am working on fuchsia and black! Each section can be as big as what I have fabrics for.

Since both greens have black and fuchsia, it doesn't matter whether I put black or fuchsia first. The line could be green, black (RP), fuchsia, or it could be green, fuchsia (RP), and black.

Green fabric that features other colors can then lead the path in a new direction.

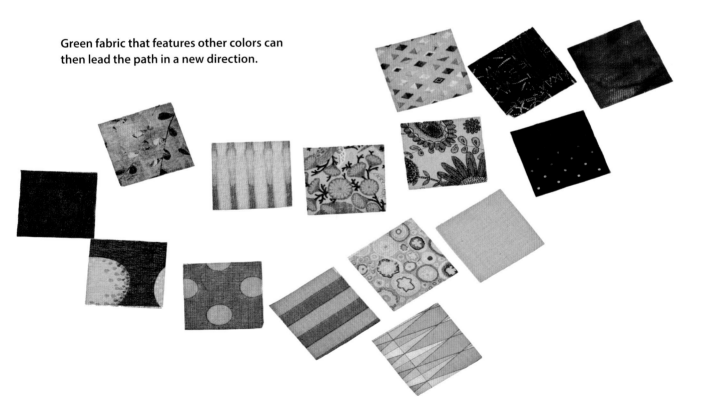

ANOTHER ALTERNATE ROUTE

Let's say instead of teal I want to use dark blue, just because I have done that in previous projects and think blue looks good with purple and green. It does! But without having any fabric that can make a connection to the green and purple, it will be a stranger in my work. There is no connection, and I can't use blue until I find a way to make a connection. I can't do what I want; I must listen to the fabric and see if it gives me an opening to use blue.

Let's do the same method again. I found a purple-with-blue fabric, but it cannot go in between the purple and the mainly purple with some green. It also can't be in the line purple and teal, where it has no connection. It needs to go in another direction while starting near purple.

Next, I found a fabric that has purple, blue, green, and many other colors in it. This fabric is my RP because it has purple and green, meaning the purple-blue fabric should lay closer to the purple. The fabric with only blue and green needs to be closer to green. Blue can be somewhere in the middle, close to the RP. My line on that side has become purple, purple/blue, purple/blue/green, blue, blue/green, green. A third line!

Can you see how coral can be picked up in the fabric with purple, green, and blue, introducing a new color to my work? This works as long as I keep it away from the purple-and-green line because none of these fabrics have any coral in them.

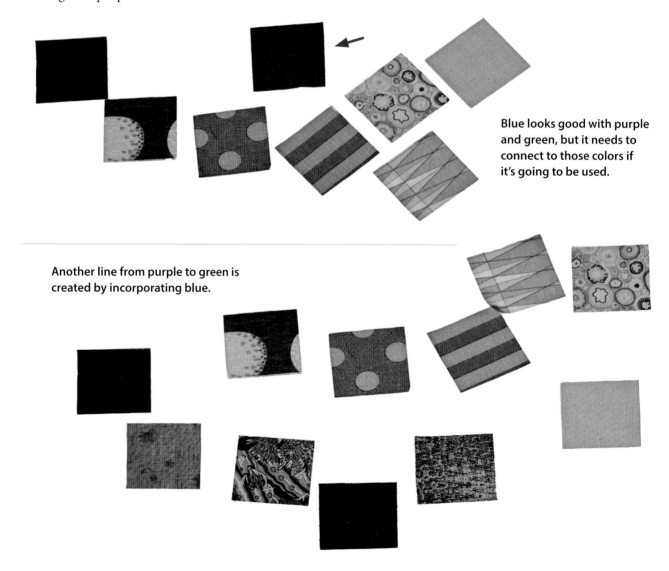

Blue looks good with purple and green, but it needs to connect to those colors if it's going to be used.

Another line from purple to green is created by incorporating blue.

Example 2: Gray to Orange

I put my gray down, I put my orange down, and in between I have to come up with fabrics that link these two colors together. I can't just look for all kinds of grays or all kinds of oranges. That would not make a connection between them. I need to find a gray-with-orange or an orange-with-gray fabric, and I will create the relationship by putting such a fabric in between them. This can be the middle, but it doesn't have to be exactly in the middle. For example, the fabric can be orange with tiny gray dots. All other fabrics I find now have a reference point. That means I compare them with my reference point. A fabric with more orange needs to go between my RP and the orange. If more gray than my RP, it needs to stay close to gray.

Now I am trying to find more fabrics, as I want my path to be longer. All those fabrics need to be either:

- The same color gray and/or orange, whether that means the main color of the fabric is gray/orange or it reads as gray/orange.
- A bit darker or lighter than gray and/or orange.

When looking for more fabrics, you are welcome to add lighter and darker shades of the exact same color gray/orange to the line. It must be close to the same shade. Another color gray (green-gray, purplish) is considered another color and a stranger. It needs to make its own line. Another tint of orange is also not welcome. Only shades that have my color gray and/or orange should be used. I am adding the color white to my line because it's a neutral that does not introduce a new, strange color.

 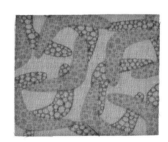 

The Connector may end up closer to orange because the gray is not as close to black as needed.

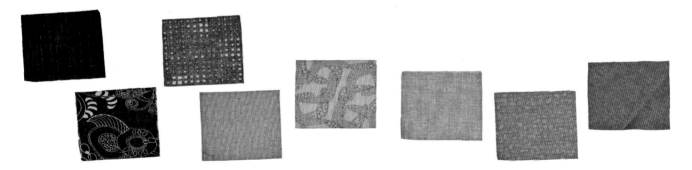

The line can expand on either end of your starting colors as well as in between.

CONNECTING WITH COLOR

I can also make my gray-orange line with the help of another color. I found an aqua that has gray and orange, which will make a good reference point. Fabrics with gray/aqua need to go in between gray and aqua; fabrics with orange/aqua need to go in between orange and aqua. The aqua star print is a toss-up. I put it on the left side of the aqua because it is a lighter fabric, and I think that transition from light gray to light blue is better than on the other side of the aqua.

In general, when you are in doubt and you see two possibilities, put the fabrics of one color from dark to light and use your phone to check. It almost always gives you an answer.

Another way to make the gray-to-orange line is with the help of some pink that I have found. The pink with gray and orange is my RP and will determine where everything has to go. All the grays stay together, all the oranges stay together. On purpose, I am arranging these fabrics a little casually because we are making pathways, clusters of colors, and not rigid lines.

The orange with pink has a little bit of dark green in it. I can pick up that color and expand my path into a different direction if I want.

Conclusion: Any color can get connected to another color. You don't need to know color theories or the color wheel. You just have to look closely at your fabrics, making sure that the pieces of fabric have something in common. Without a link, a fabric can't be used. There is not much choice in choosing where to put a fabric because the line will tell you where it has to be when you compare the fabrics.

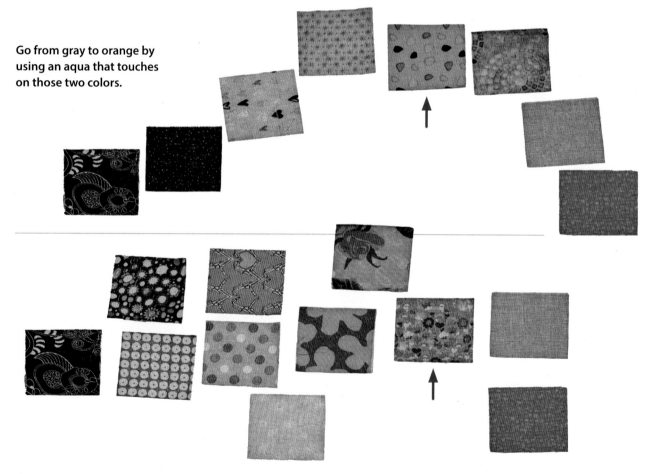

Go from gray to orange by using an aqua that touches on those two colors.

This connection using dark pink also picks up light pink and yellow that could lead to other paths.

Preparing Fabrics

Collage is a form of raw-edge appliqué. You will need lots of little pieces of fabric, and all these fabrics need to have some fusible on the wrong side of the fabric. At the very end of the creative process, this fusible will attach the fabrics permanently to the background. The fusible Lite Steam-A-Seam 2 (LSAS2) is your glue.

If you have never used LSAS2 before, it may be helpful to know that you will iron twice in the process.

1. You will iron the fusible to the wrong side of the fabric. You are applying "glue" to the fabric. LSAS2 is not just any glue but a special kind that allows you to place the fabric, then reposition it without it losing any stickiness. It's almost a way to turn your fabric into a sticker.

2. Once you are completely done and happy with your layout, only then do you press the collage. This heat will activate the adhesive and make your work permanent. Your glue will do its job. Once your pieces are secured with heat, you cannot move them again without damaging your collage.

As a rule, use your iron to attach the fusible to the fabrics, but then keep it far away from your work until you are completely satisfied.

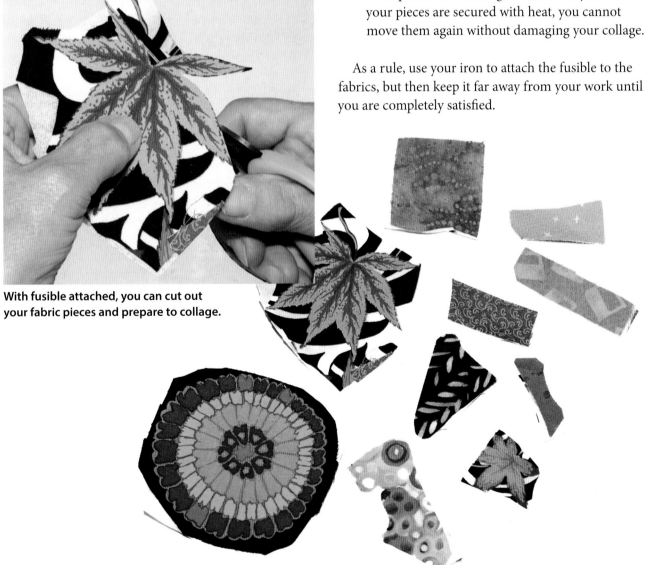

With fusible attached, you can cut out your fabric pieces and prepare to collage.

How to Use Fusible

Let's look at the fusible web. It has a grid on one side. For our purposes, you can ignore this grid; we won't use it. If you fold the release paper slightly away, without removing it, you will now see two sides. One side has a certain stickiness to it that you can feel with your fingers. This stickiness is the glue. The other side is smooth.

You can prepare each piece of fabric individually, but in general, it is easier to select several fabrics you plan to use and place them on the fusible at the same time. In the entire collage process, LSAS2 is the most expensive notion you need, and you'll want to make the best use of it. Therefore, you want to place the fabrics as closely to each other as possible.

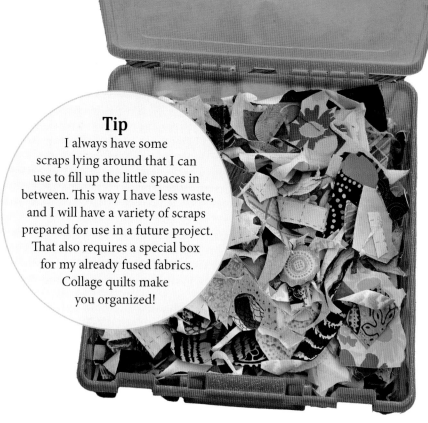

Tip

I always have some scraps lying around that I can use to fill up the little spaces in between. This way I have less waste, and I will have a variety of scraps prepared for use in a future project. That also requires a special box for my already fused fabrics. Collage quilts make you organized!

Keep scraps on hand that can fill in the spaces on your fusible.

1. Put the fusible on an ironing board with the sticky side up. Lift the release paper a little. Place the wrong side of the fabrics onto the fusible. Place them closely together so almost all the stickiness is covered on the fusible, but **do not** overlap your fabrics. If you overlap pieces, the top one will get no glue, as it is instead touching the bottom fabric.

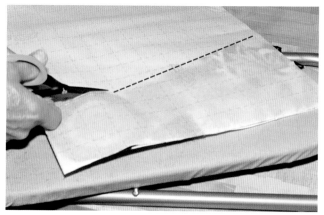

2. Fold the release paper back down. Cut the section of fusible from the roll close to where you've applied your fabric pieces.

Tip

Always cut out your fabric a little bit more generously *before* you apply the fusible web. In other words, if you plan to use a specific flower shape, put a border around it for preparing with fusible. One you've added your fusible, you can cut it to the exact size. This ensures that the fusible reaches to the edges of your fabric cuts. If you cut it to the exact size, your edges may miss some fusible, which can result in fraying later on.

It's better to start with extra border fabric, which you can cut down later.

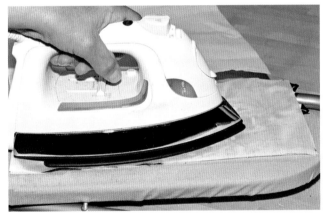

3. Press with a heated iron directly on top of the release paper. The heat will activate the fusible and apply it to the fabric. Place the iron just long enough for the fusible to attach to the fabric, about six seconds; your iron might take a shorter or longer time. Don't move the iron back and forth, just press.

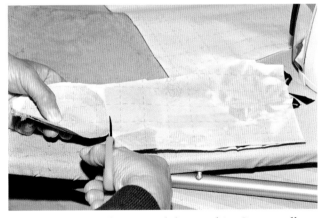

4. Let the pressed unit cool down a bit. Cut out all the pieces one by one. You can cut with the release paper on or without it. I do both but tend to remove the paper when the cutting is more intricate. If you are cutting through paper, be mindful of the scissors you choose.

I started by laying down the "winners" to get an idea of the overall composition.

Find Your Process When Preparing Fabrics

At the start of each collage, I am usually much more intuitive when selecting my fabrics to prepare. I look for fabrics that I think may work for what I have in mind in at least three colors. I make a pile of winners and one labeled "maybe." I apply fusible web to the winners, setting aside the maybe pile.

Once my pieces are prepared and cut, I place all my winners on my foundation (either Pattern Ease or a neutral fabric), grouping the same colors together more or less. If I already see a connection, I try to honor that. Nothing too serious, because I can change everything. Rather than working on each line individually, I work on many lines at the same time and fill spots as I go, replace, and fill more.

As the collage develops, I may revisit my Maybe pile, prepare more fabrics, and continue. For me, every quilt comes together differently. Sometimes I know exactly what I am doing, sometimes I'm searching.

Cutting Fabrics

After your fabric is fused, you can cut the Leaders and the Kisses out according to their shape. You selected these fabrics for their shapes, so now you cut your pieces by following the design of the fabric.

Cutting Leaders

On the opposite pageXX is a blue print that I chose for a Leader. I cut out the flower roughly with some extra fabric around it. After the fusible has been attached, I can cut the exact shape of the flower.

Follow the lines the best you can, but it is not necessary to cut each tiny little detail. Sometimes flowers have tiny little edges, which you can cut around more roughly. It is up to you how detailed you want to be. The shape is just a guide.

The reason I'm not too strict here is that later, when I free motion quilt all the edges, tiny little details disappear in my stitching anyway. If I think my free motion quilting can keep the details visible, I can cut those out as well. If not, I will cut them off now.

Cut the Leader out based on the shape given to you.

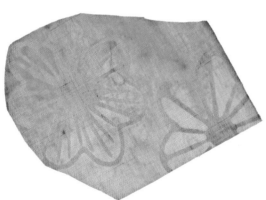

Here you can see the full design and the partial design. The partial is still good to use.

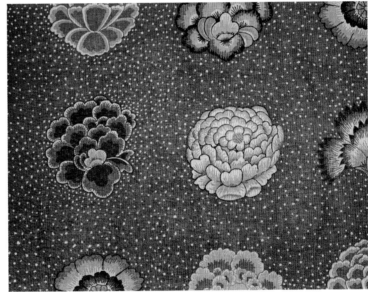

Seven of the nine flowers are cut off, but they can still be used as Leaders.

Often, you'll find a fabric in your stash that has the potential to be a Leader, but part of the shape is missing. It happens more than you'd think! For instance, you cut in the middle of a flower, and instead of having a nice round flower, only one side of its circle is left. No problem. These partial-Leader shapes are still of great use.

Similarly, some brand-new cuts only have half of a motif at the edge. The brown fabric above is a fat quarter, but many of the flowers are partial. When

placing the fabrics, we will pretend as if the missing part is underneath another fabric. There you will see how partial Leaders give your work depth by playing a little peek-a-boo. For now, just know that this is a valuable piece of fabric.

Note: These kinds of scraps often come from other quilt projects. Many people toss them out, but as you can see, this little leftover is giving me two good Leaders.

Similar to Leaders, trim Kisses to the exact shape.

Cutting Kisses

Kisses are little shapes, and you will try to cut those out as well, as precisely as you can.

The fabric above has several possibilities for Kisses. I want to use two of them and cut them out together (since they are close anyway), leaving some extra space around. After the fusible has cooled off, I trim the flowers to the shape presented. There is less leeway with Kisses, so try to be careful when cutting.

Cutting Followers and Connectors

Cutting out Followers and Connectors is vaguer, as you don't have a line to follow. The fabric has no design with a shape. You yourself are creating a shape.

In general, try to cut without any straight lines and no sharp edges. I know this is not what you have learned elsewhere in cutting fabrics! We are so used to cutting ¼" (6.4mm) and precise points; now I'm asking you to let all that go. Cut like a little child learning to work with scissors, and make complete random shapes. The reason to do it this way is that you are trying to avoid straight lines and sharp points. Those don't connect well. Sharp points don't make friends. Softer shapes create smoother edges, and this will help to make your lines look natural. The

eyes can follow the flow easier when there are no straight lines.

Followers and Connectors should be cut in such a way that they will allow room for the Leaders to shine. That means, to achieve proper balance in your work, Followers and Connectors are cut mostly smaller than the Leaders they surround. Sometimes you can cut them in about the same size, but a 3" (7.6cm) Leader in between 5" (12.7cm) Followers will turn into a Kiss. The dimensions are wrong. They are out of proportion.

In general, I would cut Followers and Connectors roughly between 1½"–3" (3.8–7.6cm). That is, if you have a choice. Some scraps are 1" (2.5cm) and those are perfect to use. It is nice to have a variety of sizes available. Even ½" (1.3cm) scraps are fine. If you have a jelly roll leftover, it will be 2½" (6.4cm) wide. Some people just prefer bigger pieces and will cut to 3" or 4" (7.6 or 10.2cm). Later, they will probably cut them smaller and create new leftovers, so I would rather be frugal at the beginning. Every piece will need to get fusible web, and you will go quickly through it if all the pieces are generous.

If it is a brand-new piece of fabric, or a piece coming from a bigger scrap, cut a rectangle about 2" x 3" (5.1 x 7.6cm). That will be plenty for most Followers

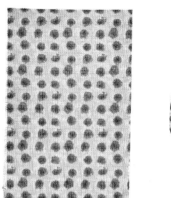

Cut a 2" x 3" (5.1 x 7.6cm) rectangle, then cut it again into an organic shape.

and Connectors. You don't have to measure anything. All this cutting goes freestyle. With a pair of scissors, cut curvy pieces by eye. Relax, it will be fine. You can always cut it smaller, funkier, or curvier later. I almost always have to give my Followers and Connectors little cuts later. By then, I can see where its position will be, and I will give the fabric a little trim. Easy enough. You can also add another piece of the same fabric to your work if it was cut too small. You simply can't go wrong!

Cutting Multiple Pieces

Sometimes one fabric will have a lot of possibilities for Leaders, Connectors, and Kisses. I applied fusible on the back of the fat quarter below and started cutting. The big flower has detailed petals. I could cut these out, but I decided to not use them for my Leader; instead, making it a big round shape is enough.

I cut a very tiny Kiss and some other sections that could become Connectors or Kisses at a later time. You always have the option to cut fabrics smaller at a later time when you have a better idea where you will use them in your work.

Proportion

Sometimes a designer has a huge flower in the collection, and if you want to use this big shape as a Leader, your Followers and Connectors must be bigger as well. Think about how such a huge section will look in your entire work because it will make everything else look small and out of proportion. A much better way to proceed is to use only part of that big flower. It will still give you an interesting shape without overpowering everything.

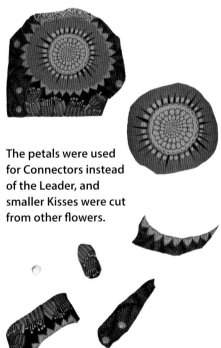

The petals were used for Connectors instead of the Leader, and smaller Kisses were cut from other flowers.

These flowers are too large, even for a Leader.

This print, Cactus Flower by Philip Jacobs, has flowers that are 8" x 8" (20.3 x 20.3cm). Way too big for a collage! You can cut such a flower in thirds, quarters, or even smaller pieces and use only one of those smaller sections of the big flower. The advantage is that you still get some of the effect of the large design, but it is not overpowering everything else.

In this example, I split the flower into five Leaders, though it could be broken even further into Followers, Connectors, or Kisses. I also saved the little pieces with fusible that came off with the cutting. I may or may not use those later, but for now I'll save them.

Since the cutting of fabric is such a relaxing activity, I sometimes do this at those moments in the day when I feel too tired or too rushed to do a more demanding job. I can still work the fabric, but I don't have to do any precision work!

When all your fabrics are backed with fusible and cut to their shape (exact for Leaders and Kisses or random for Followers and Connectors), the placing of fabrics can start. No doubt you will be fusing more very, very soon.

Because of the flower's size, the petals can still make for good Leaders.

Placing Fabrics

Finally, we've come to the really fun part: placing all our fabrics. You may find you've selected and prepared every piece you need to create the collage you had envisioned, but more often than not, especially when it comes to Kisses, you'll find your design taking on a mind of its own, and you'll be head back to the ironing board to prepare some additional fabrics. You can always cut more fabrics as you go.

With these cut pieces, you can now arrange lines and paths on the background.

Getting Started

First, we need to find a background for all the fabric pieces, a foundation. As mentioned, I prefer to work with Pattern Ease. This lightweight paper is an economic choice, sturdy enough, stays in the quilt, and doesn't create any issues with quilting later on.

Cut a piece of fabric a little bit bigger than the size you have in mind for your project. Pattern Ease is 46" (116.8cm) wide; for your first projects, I recommend you cut it in half. That will still let you make something as big as 18" x 23" (45.7 x 58.4cm).

I usually cut my foundation in the size that fits my design board and start with the 46" (116.8cm) width.

I can always make it smaller, but that hardly ever happens. The space gives me more room to let the colors do their magic.

You can also work directly on a piece of fabric that is not Pattern Ease. Just make sure this fabric is neutral, light color, medium weight, and without any loud designs. You wouldn't want to see the design of your background fabric shining through the collage pieces—unless, of course, it is intentional. Using a colored background allows you to leave some spots uncovered.

The gray background occasionally, and intentionally, peeks through the collage on this piece.

Techniques

A blank piece of foundation paper is looking at you, and you are staring at it. Let's combine our knowledge of fabric categories with our knowledge of making paths. We want the color to form a starting line, and we will use the fabric categories as a guide.

It is always helpful to have three main colors in your mind before you start. You probably will add more colors later on, but three colors are a good start. In each of those three colors, you should have some Leaders ready to go, some Followers, and some Connectors are great as well, if you know what you are looking for.

Kisses can be cut, and often are when you see them, but they won't be applied until the end. They come in handy to fill little openings on the Lite Steam-A-Seam 2 (LSAS2) when fusing all your other fabrics, so I prepare what I think I might need. The more you practice this technique, the better you'll become at preparing just the right Kisses in advance.

When I see an interesting Connector with the possible color of a Leader, I give it some fusible and put it close to my work. There is value in a fabric with many possible Connectors, so preparing some of it in advance may keep you from having to go back and work with additional fabrics.

Lesson 1: A Basic Line (Leader, Follower, Leader)

A very basic line is Leader 1 and Leader 2. This happens when you are working with fabrics in the same color. One Leader is darker than the other Leader. If you want to travel from a darker color to a lighter color, no Connectors are needed. You could still have Followers in between. These Followers are going from dark to light as well.

Once you've established your line, you can then more creatively place your fabric, following the order you established. They can be placed wherever you want as long as they follow the direction of the Leaders, showing as much or as little of your Followers as you like.

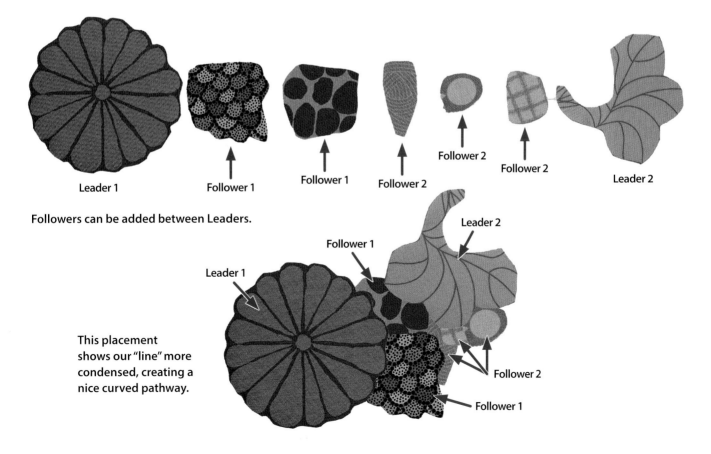

Leader 1   Follower 1   Follower 1   Follower 2   Follower 2   Follower 2   Leader 2

Followers can be added between Leaders.

Follower 1   Leader 2   Leader 1   Follower 2   Follower 1

This placement shows our "line" more condensed, creating a nice curved pathway.

You may be asking why I'm not labeling my Followers consecutively (Follower 1, Follower 2, Follower 3, Follower 4, etc.). Lesson 3 will make this much clearer, but keep in mind that I'm numbering as a teaching tool. It's not something you'll actively do as you build your collages.

WHAT IF YOU HAVE TWO LEADERS THAT ARE THE SAME COLOR?

The first thing to check is to see that these are not the same fabric. In general, duplicating a fabric is a no-no, unless you have really good reasons for doing it. For instance, you are making a collage for someone with a fabric that has special meaning to this person. The same fabric could be used elsewhere in the quilt, but not next to each other. It would draw too much attention. Leader 3 and Leader 15 could be the same fabric, but they are at different spots in the quilt.

The line should go from bigger to smaller with three Leaders of the same color.

If they are different fabrics, you need to look closely to confirm that these are indeed the same colors. If they are the same or very close colors, it is the size of the Leader that will determine the line order. A bigger Leader comes before a smaller Leader. I would not recommend putting Leaders of the same color too closely together without any Followers in between to break up the similarity a little. It would create one big red spot in the quilt.

Lesson 2: Adding a Connector (Leader, Connector, Leader)

What if we want to add another color to link two different colors? As you learned previously, a Connector will have more than one color, and in that mix, one color must match Leader 1 and one color must match Leader 2. In our scenario, the blue flower on the left is Leader 1, the red-and-blue spots is our Connector, and the red flower is Leader 2.

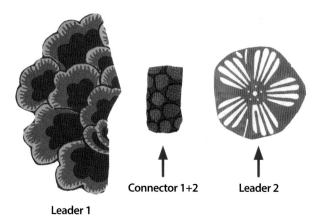

Connector 1+2   Leader 2

Leader 1

A Connector brings Leaders together because it carries the colors of each.

You might find the colors that you need for your Connector in a piece of fabric that has a certain shape. If this shape is larger than 1" (2.5cm), it is a Leader; if it is smaller than 1" (2.5cm), it is a Kiss. Either way, you are using it as a Connector. This is one of the areas where a fabric can be both at the same time.

Lesson 3: Expanding Your Line with Followers

Slowly but surely, you are learning to expand the path by adding Followers and Connectors between the Leaders. The key is color. Make sure each Follower is linked to both its Leader and the Connector between. Follower 1 is linked to Leader 1. Follower 2 is linked to Leader 2. Both are linked to the Connector, thus the Connector here is labeled 1+2.

Note: For learning purposes, we're only mentally "numbering" our Followers and Connectors. As you start to add more, numbering them in relation to your Leaders might be more confusing than it is helpful. What's most important is the links between the colors and the smooth transition from one to the other.

Here is an expanded version of the previous pathway, leaning more heavily toward red, as we've added several red Followers. They're all labeled Follower 2 because of their relation to Leader 2. The amount of suitable fabric that can be applied to a line will determine how big a line will become. I found five reds that could work, creating this path: blue Leader, blue Follower, blue/red Connector, 5 red Followers, and red Leader.

Lesson 4: Arranging Followers

So you're flush in red Followers and ready to take off in that direction, but how exactly do you order them? Let your fabrics be you your guide. My Leader 2 has red and white in it, so in the previous lesson, I placed the red Followers that read the most white closest to Leader 2. The Followers that are only red stayed closer to the Connector, which has no white in it at all.

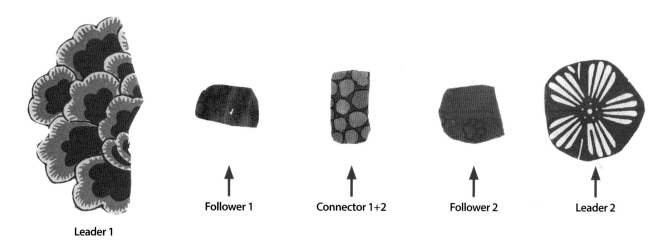

Leader 1   Follower 1   Connector 1+2   Follower 2   Leader 2

The Followers can also be brought together by the Connector.

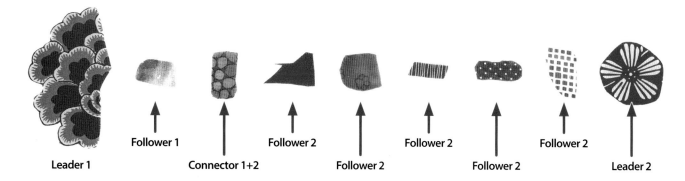

Leader 1   Follower 1   Connector 1+2   Follower 2   Follower 2   Follower 2   Follower 2   Follower 2   Leader 2

Lengthen the line in any direction depending on the colors you have.

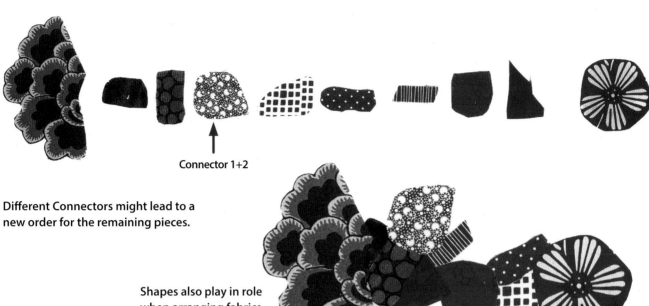

Connector 1+2

Different Connectors might lead to a new order for the remaining pieces.

Shapes also play in role when arranging fabrics in a path.

However, look how that changes when I add one extra blue-and-red Connector with a touch of white in it. Now the argument that the red-and-white Followers need to stay close to Leader 2 is less valid. The pieces with more white now make more sense near the Connector, continuing the line from lighter to darker to match the red of Leader 2.

But the order of colors really isn't a hard-and-fast rule. Why? Because ultimately, you won't be placing your fabrics in this straight line—remember, we avoid straight lines in freestyle color collage.

Once you start layering your pieces, they will be grouped as the colors and the shapes dictate. As it so happens, when I grouped my pieces, the red-and-white Followers did end up closer to my Leader 2. Be open to the directions your fabrics and shapes take you.

Lesson 5: Layering Pieces

Notice that *every line always starts with a Leader*. They are the most important fabrics. Everything else falls in place around them by applying the line rules:

1. Your first two pieces should be the Leader 1 (L1) and Follower 1 (F1). Remove the release paper from your pieces and place the Leader where you'd like to begin. Slightly overlap your Follower.

2. Check your overlap. If your overlap is too generous, you will not only end up with a very dense project, but you'll also waste fabric, possibly covering more of a fabric that could otherwise add to your pathway. Too little overlap

Tip
The release paper should come off easily. Sometimes a little scratch with a pin will help it to come off. If it is harder to get it off, it means you didn't iron it long enough. Go back to your ironing board and press the fabric a little bit longer. That should solve the problem.

Here, the overlap is correct, but these colors do not match and should not be placed together.

This placement has too much overlap. Fabric is wasted.

This placement does not have enough overlap. There are little holes.

will leave you with a lot of holes, creating a need for many Kisses and leading to a somewhat messy result.

3. Continue to build your collage. You will find that your Followers, no matter when you put them on your work, should end up under your Leader and Connectors. With that in mind, don't let Connectors overshadow your Leaders. Generally, Leaders trump Connectors, and Connectors trump Followers. But follow your instincts. In the case of "partial Leaders," you'll want the incomplete side to lie underneath another fabric, which could be a Follower or a Connector.

4. Keep your scissors handy, especially when you are placing Followers and Connectors. You may have to adjust the piece and make it smaller, because you don't want too much fabric to lay under another piece. It could be too big when you have a smaller Leader. Or it could be that your curve should be a little softer or funkier.

LAYERING EXAMPLE

Let's give layering a try as we create this small collage section.

a. Begin with a partial Leader. In this case, a white flower.

b. Cover the "bad" side with some fabrics. The partial Leader is placed first, then two Followers are laid on top. I put the darkest on top, but you could also put the stripe fabric on top.

c. Add another Follower. In this case, I placed it underneath my Leader and one of the Followers.

d. In this example, I'm showing you how *not* to place fabrics. I positioned a second Leader (L2) on top of my first Leader (L1). As you can see, it pulls the focus away from the first Leader. Avoid placing Leaders on Leaders.

e. Place at least one Follower in between and underneath L1 and L2.

f. Continue building the collage. I added a Connector on top of my two original Followers. This fabric is a Connector because it brings in a different color, dark blue.

Lesson 6: Placing and Building

Place an L1 on your surface, not in the exact middle and not along the very edges. L1 is the beginning of your work, and you want to have room to expand out from it. Remember, once you start building, we can move our L1 if we feel the pathway moving in a different direction, as long as nothing has been pressed down.

If you have multiple Followers, they can be put in a row, moving away from the Leader. Or you can place multiple Followers around the Leader. Since these fabrics are equal in value, you can decide which ones you like best and put those on top. In the student's work shown below, she slightly encircled her L1 and worked toward her L2, which is the cluster of the orange daisies.

Opposite the yellow-orange pathway, however, this student has added a blue circle to serve as her L3. Her goal now is to link the fabrics together with yellow-and-blue Connectors and coordinating Followers.

Keep in mind that the distance between L1 and L2 is random and determined by the number of Followers and Connectors you plan to use. It can

Remember the Rules

Here is a recap of what we have learned:

- After placing L1 and L2, the fabrics between L1 and L2 have to follow certain line rules.

- Ideally, there should be at least one Connector between L1 and L2. If not, L2 needs to be lighter or darker in value than L1.

- A Follower that has a higher percentage of color L1 than of color L2, has to be placed closer to L1

- A Follower that has a higher percentage of color L2 than of color L1, has to be placed closer to L2.

- A Connector that has a higher percentage of color L1 than of color L2 has to be placed closer to L1.

- A Connector that has a higher percentage of color L2 than of color L1, has to be placed closer to L2.

Strictly following these instructions, which requires more rational than artistic thinking, will lead to a nice flow in your work.

My student chose the large yellow flower as her L1, placing it off center before adding more elements.

be 1" (2.5cm), it can be 8" (20.3cm), or it can be somewhere in between. Continuing with this example, the distance between L1 and L2 is much shorter than the distance between L1 and L3. Spacing fabric out longer than 8" (20.3cm) before you encounter another Leader is atypical but can happen.

Your work will take the look of a constellation with lines going in different directions. You could go from L1 to L2, then repeat, going from L2 to L3 and L3 to L4. Or you could make L3 coming from another side of L1 as in the case of the student example. The number is not so important. It is more about going from Leader to Leader. You can place any Leader wherever you want, but you will need to build the connections between.

If you're doing freestyle color collage correctly, you will have a reason for putting every fabric in its place. What is the connection with a previous piece? Is it expanding our color line or moving the line toward another color? Each fabric plays a role.

Lesson 7: You're Stuck

What if your selection of prepared Followers and Connectors doesn't offer the right color mix to build a bridge between your chosen Leaders?

You have two options:

OPTION A: GO BACK TO YOUR FABRIC STASH

The way you are looking at fabric will change for the rest of your sewing life. You know the color you need, and it is a matter of finding a good match. Doesn't matter where it is coming from. I love seeing this stage in students. Suddenly they no longer think in the general quilting qualifications like modern, favorite designer, latest of the latest, or old scrap. It doesn't matter what they like, it's about what they need: color! All they need is something in a particular color, and the "ugliest" fabric may give it to them!

This grouping of fabric is a great example of how my student selected a color scheme of purples, blues, and teals, but got stuck because she couldn't find enough fabric in that family.

The solution? She started looking for any fabric that included teal, one of her Leader colors. Suddenly she saw how many teal fabrics also had green in

In trying to bridge two colors together, you might find new colors to add to your palette.

them. Lime green, in particular, was totally not on her radar, but it worked beautifully! She put the blues and purples to the side and continued to work with the lime greens.

As she built her work toward the lime greens, she found fabrics with gray and lime green and teal as well as teal with grey. Without having to do anything special, the student's work has much more contrast.

Remember, when you put your beginning Leaders on the foundation, the placement is completely random. At the end of a long day of collage, the student discovered that her problem was solved if she took off all the blues and replaced them at another spot on the foundation. Maybe it is easier to get from grey to blues with the fabrics in her stash? Nobody knows, because nobody knows her fabrics. It's a total surprise what the fabric will tell.

OPTION B: PICK A DIFFERENT LEADER

If you really can't find the right color in a Follower or Connector, not even with the help of another color, the only other option is to remove the second Leader from your plan. You have no room for this fabric yet. It is beautiful, it has a nice shape, you love the color, but you can't use it until you find a Connector.

The goal is always to make a line. If you can't build a line between L1 and L2, L2 is not meant to be in your work, at least not yet.

Lesson 8: Applying Kisses

Kisses can be applied after all the other fabrics are in place, and they play a vital role.

- Kisses can fill gaps between other pieces.
- Kisses can make "boring" Followers come alive.
- Kisses are very useful when you have more Followers than Leaders in a certain area.
- Kisses give some whimsy when points of curved cutting meet each other and turn into a point or dead zone. A Kiss on top will soften this section.
- Kisses can make you smile. A Kiss can be a little dragonfly, almost like a tattoo.
- In a serious work of color, Kisses add humor. They are just cute!

Kisses don't look too impactful on their own, but they can polish off a piece perfectly.

Lesson 9: Common Issues

In this lesson, I'm going to walk you through making some paths, showing off some common mistakes that I have run into, whether for my own work or with students. As you work through your own collage, some fabrics or connections may trip you up. I hope you see parallels to those issues in these examples, and my suggestions for what to do will help you look at your work with fresh eyes.

EXAMPLE 1

On the left, this is how connections should not be done. I can't use any of these greens—they don't do anything for my Leader. I will have to select those greens that are close in color to my Leader. See how, on the right, only the greens that pick up the color close to my Leader can be used. Everything else has to be put aside until I can make a connection to those shades of green.

EXAMPLE 2

I found a piece of fabric with the right shade dark green, moss green, and gray. This piece is the Connector to the moss greens that now can be used. All other greens still cannot be used, as they don't have a Connector. What's wrong in this picture? The pieces are cut with straight lines, sharp points. It is a line, but without organic shapes, they do not move as smoothly from one color to another.

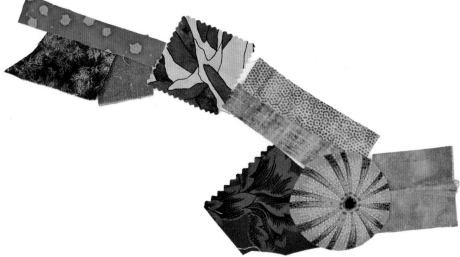

EXAMPLE 3

Looking at the top image, you can now really see a path from my original green Leader (L1) to the new olive Leader (L2). In this picture, the cutting of the Leaders is correct, as their shapes have been followed. The cutting of the Followers and Connector still looks too straight. Another problem: the darkest green Follower (F1) is bigger than its Leader. The moss green fabric (F2) is also out of proportion.

In the bottom image, some serious trimming has happened, and my pieces connect much better. Some more trimming can be done once I know the pieces of fabric that are coming next, but this is a good start. What a difference this cutting makes!

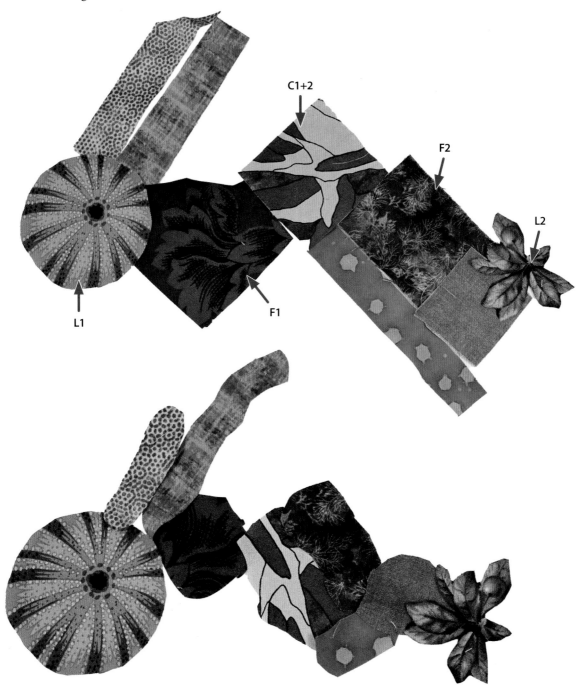

EXAMPLE 4

As you can see, I picked up the gray from the Connector and expanded my little collage toward gray. The colors are in the right order. Only problem here: The gray circle Leader (L3) happens to be very much the same size as the green circle Leader (L1), which makes the piece look flat rather than natural. Therefore, I added an even bigger Leader (L4) to make it less obvious. Once this collage gets bigger, it no longer stands out.

See how I expanded the dark green Followers? Initially, I thought I had so many greens! Turns out, I could use only some of them and needed more. All these Followers are in the same green color family—they are almost the same, but still different fabrics. The better you can do this, the more beautiful your collage will become. In every quilt there are many more Followers than Leaders, but most people have no idea. These Followers do their job of separating Leaders and expanding the total green section within the collage. They are doing a good job in supporting the Leaders. The number of Followers you need is completely a matter of taste. You could make the collage more compact; you could space it out. It's up to the eye of the artist. Very often, the availability of fabric determines how wide we can make a section.

EXAMPLE 5

The only thing I would change from Example 4 is the green Kiss. It is sitting very close to the Leader and is not adding anything to it. I removed the Kiss and put it on top of the dark green area. There, the contrast creates a little "pop." It makes a playful introduction to the brighter greens. It helps your eyes go towards the green Leader (the arrow is really a coincidence!). You could find many spots for this Kiss. If the collage is much larger, it could go even onto the gray section.

Lesson 10: Creating a Collage Step-by-Step

In this example, I will take you on the journey of making one small collage. It will end up around 18" x 20" (45.7 x 50.8cm). I have numbered the most important Leaders. This way, you can see the different sections and lines better.

1. Build from L1 to L2. I used my sample from Lesson 4 as my first line. Note the little pins that label 1 for L1 and 2 for L2.

2. Build from L1 to L3. I am giving the blue-and-white flower the label L3 and placing it closer to L1 because it is near the blue side of L1–L2 line. I didn't have to do this. I could have easily gone another way and started with L3 anywhere else. A sample of artistic freedom! In between L1 and L3 are Followers in white and blue.

3. Build from L3 to L4. In the left corner is L4, which is darker than L3. Its Followers are darker than F3.

4. Expand L1 and L2. I have found a fun fish fabric with red-and-blue stripes. It works as another Connector between L1 and L2. Because it has a notable shape, it becomes a new Leader (L5).

5. Build on L5. This new Leader has a medium blue that I will pick up. I added four medium blue Followers; they are in the same color, so the biggest ones come first.

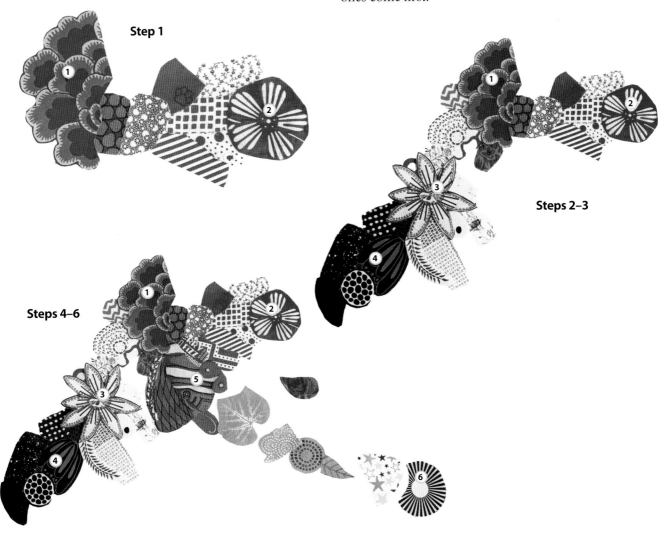

Step 1

Steps 2–3

Steps 4–6

6. Adding L6. The line changes to another shade of dark blue, moving to a new Leader. How could it do this? Because of the star fabric that is the Connector. This white print happens to be white, but it is the blues that do the work. (It could also give an opening to a new section with whites.)

7. Fill in the sections. The space in between L4, L5, and L6 needs to get filled up by fabrics that make connections to all these points. I decided to give the bottom of the quilt all darker blues, connecting L4 with L6. On this line is an important piece with white and lighter blues, which makes it possible to go from L4 in a curve to L5. In between is a partial blue sunflower that is covered on its bad side.

8. Expand L6. I add darker blues for the corner and make my way up with whites and darker blues. The red pinwheel fabric is an early Kiss that I am using as a reminder to look for slightly darker reds.

9. Expand L2 to L6. I start with slightly darker reds and combine them with darker blues. The line more or less follows the medium blues. A red-and-white star on top of everything ties multiple fabric pieces together.

10. Adding L7. This is a lighter blue fabric with red. It gives direction to this entire area that can be red or light blue. Light blue is lighter than the medium blues in between L5 and L6, so slowly the newer fabrics are becoming lighter, though some red-with-blue Connectors (which have to stay closer to the reds) can be worked in as well. There are several light blue Leaders.

Step 7

Steps 8–10

11. Adding L8. When placing the new Leader, it changes the red to a more orange red and the light blue to a more cobalt blue. Thanks to some good Connectors, I could push the aqua and orangey color all the way into the right corner.

12. Adding L9. This changes the blue into another tint. I fill up the area with more aquas, though keeping some darker blue with red on the lower end. The darker blues find their origin in L1, which is a good Connector to blue and aqua.

13. Adding L10. A purple-blue color is coming in. This color is first combined with the aqua, but it moves into the color of L1.

Step 11

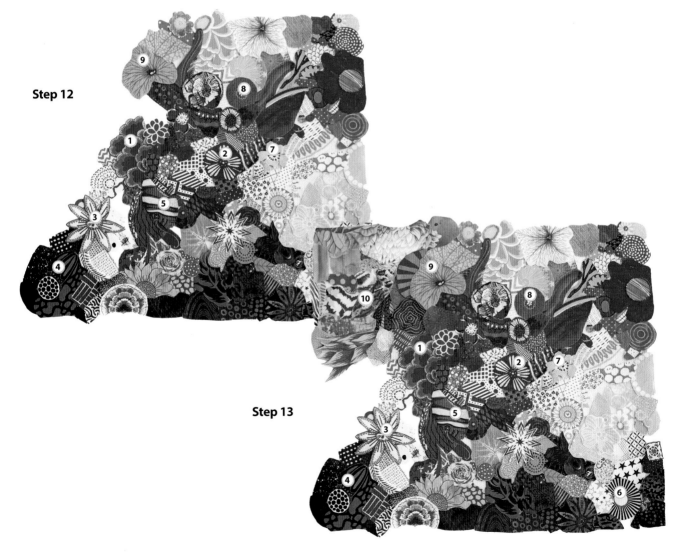

Step 12

Step 13

14. Adding L11. This Leader contributes to the slightly purple-blue area. It connects the colors of L1 and L3.

15. Apply all the Kisses. They can solve several problems, whether it's adding more of one color to an area, providing contrast, or most importantly, covering up the background peeking through.

The numbers of the Leaders are not important. L11 could have been L5 if I worked the other way around. Take a step back. Look at the piece again, and follow with your eyes along the road they naturally want to follow. You have become a better traveler!

Step 14

Step 15

Mapping a Finished Collage

Learning how to organize and arrange freestyle collages often takes a completely new mindset. It can be hard to grasp the technique right away. So here is another way of learning how to collage that might help some of you. Let's map out what links one section of this example quilt to the other. In other words, how did I build my paths from one colorway to the next?

Example 1

Look at all the different green colors in the quilt. They are separated. At the bottom right, there is dark green with black, moving into lighter green and gray. From there, the green becomes more teal, mainly thanks to some excellent gray-green-teal Connectors.

On the top left of the quilt is a bright green, which is a completely different color from what has been explored so far. Some purples introduce us to this color. Then there is lime green with teal, slowly growing into aqua. What made that possible? Kaffe Fassett's teal with lime green flower print! It's just one fabric, but plays such an important role, both as a Connector and Leader.

On the right side, you see some olive greens and muddier greens, introduced by a powerful black circle fabric, that grew out of the dark green/black. All these greens are sometimes connected to each other by gradually adding lighter shades of green, other times by Connectors introducing other colors.

"Abundance" is a sample I made using cool colors for my Houston 2023 Festival class.

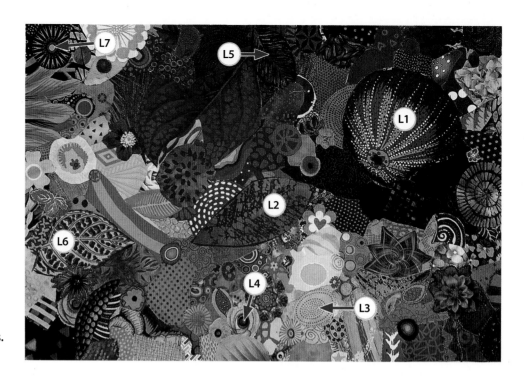

I made this example for this book as another way of training your eye to paths.

The blues are even more connected. There is dark blue, royal blue, purple-blue, green-blue—your eyes go from one grouping into the other. The colors are changing slowly with some subtle Connectors.

The purple is also connected tightly. Blue-purples make a curve and grow into red-purples then lighter shades. Look where the fabrics are with both color purples. These are the ones that connect the purple-blue to the red-purples.

What you realize as you follow the colors from one section of "Abundance" to the next is nothing is randomly placed, nor does any colorway stop abruptly where another starts. Each section slowly pours into the next with the help of Leaders, Followers, and Connectors.

Example 2

The big purple ball is 4" (10.2cm). It is my L1, with two shades of purple (red-purples and blue-purples), some dark gray, and some white. The red-purple Followers are placed close to the red-purple in the L1. The blue-purple Followers are placed close to the blue-purple in the L1. They are growing to L2, the orange-red leaf. In between the blue-purples and the L2 is a small but very important Connector.

More toward the bottom, the blue-purples are becoming lighter with some yellow. There is a purple-yellow Connector to the yellow L3. In between L2 and L3, the space gets filled with orange and yellow. At the tip of L2, bright oranges are showing up.

The blue-purple transitions into full blues in the right corner. In between the L3 and the oranges, an L4 is put down that introduces blue to the left side of this sample.

On another side of L2, a big partial Leader (L5) has been placed, moving this area toward fuchsia. In between L1 and L5 is a spot for a purple-fuchsia Connector. It is now a matter of finding more pieces of fabric that could fill the spots. The darker Followers are staying at the top. The lighter ones, with a hint of the orange L2 color in it as well, are the Followers between L2 and L5.

L4 opens the way to blues in the left corner. There are some Connectors in orange/blue, and then the blue introduces green. There is a great green-orange Connector. The big green leaf is L6, which has some lime green in it that I picked up. Lime green goes toward L5. The color green is changing slowly into a more teal green, which connects to L5 by a red/teal Connector. L6 transitions to teal but also gets surrounded with little black accents, moving to the black L7 in the top-left corner.

Finishing

After you have filled up your entire workspace with lines going from the first to the last Leader, and you are pleased with the result, it is time to make the collage permanent. Take your work carefully over to an ironing board, making sure nothing shifts, and iron your work. Apply pressure with heat directly on the fabrics; don't move your iron too much over the work. It's amazing to see what happens.

If you think you have touched every area, lift your work and hold it in front of a window. Carefully check the entire piece. You may find some little "holes": sections that have no fabric attached to them. Fill up those little pieces with fabric snippets that were created when you trimmed the edges of some pieces. Nobody will know the difference. Iron again. Once all the fabrics are fused into their permanent positions, the quilt top is ready.

There are several options for what you can do with your collage. You can do anything with your collage

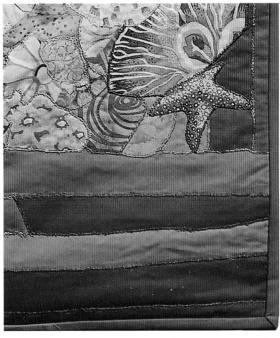

Fused borders were the perfect finish in "The Crack."

Fusing makes the fabrics blend and your work look so much more cohesive!

The collage used as a background makes for a good contrast to the solid-color flowers.

that you would do with a quilt top, such as make a pillow or table runner. However, I will suggest a few things that I personally have done. In every situation, your foundation stays in.

Option 1: You can leave it as is and finish it. This piece can become a wall hanging on its own, or it can become part of a bigger wall hanging. Your collage could be used as the center of a larger piece like a center medallion block, or you could finish it in such a way to add borders to it. You can sew or fuse borders onto it, which I did in "The Crack" (page 10).

Option 2: You can use your collage as a background to a piece, and embellish or appliqué it with other fabrics. "Growing Color" (above) is an example of flowers standing proud against a collage background. It can then be finished in any of the ways mentioned in option 1.

Use your collage like a patch on clothing, adding a beautiful, decorative element.

Option 3: You can use your collage as a fabric to cut out big sections. I mentioned in the Introduction that I cut the leaves out of my fabric "dough." You can use your collage to embellish or mend clothing, like I did with a jacket. (Option 3 is the opposite of option 2.)

Finishing on Clothing

If you want use collage to embellish or mend clothes, the technique is relatively simple. Turn your work around and draw the desired shape on the wrong side before you cut. If you happen to have a plastic template, you can place the template on the right side of the top to view your fussy cuts in advance. In a way, you are turning your collage into a regular appliqué shape.

A big orange peel template gives great cutouts. In the photo below, look at the template on the back of the collage, laying on the Pattern Ease. After tracing and cutting the peel shapes, they can be appliquéd on a regular foundation.

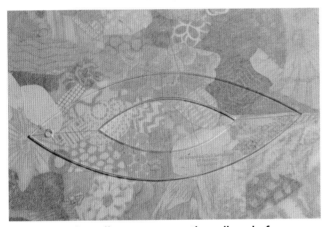

A clear template allows you to see the collage before you cut.

Cutout circles from collage always make great shapes for appliqué.

If you are cutting out your collage, it is super easy to cut everything. Once you have cut out the shape you want, lift it, and audition it on a background. It's nice to have this option, and backgrounds make such a big impact on the total look.

Once you have found a background, apply a little bit of LSAS2 on the back of your collage (to the Pattern Ease). Iron, let cool, and turn the collage around. Put it on the spot you want, iron again, and now you can sew it on just like any appliqué piece. Use a zigzag or blanket stitch to stitch it down.

Finishing as a Wall Hanging

While this section says *wall hanging*, you can use this information for making another type of quilted project. A pillow, table runner, or quilt could all be made with freestyle collage quilting.

As a note, my preferred way of backing the project is giving the collage a so-called "false back." The backing fabric is used to cover up all the threads, where normally you can see all the stitches on the back. I wouldn't have to do this if I would use only a few different threads, but my quilts have over 100 different threads. I quilt one shape and change the color of the top or the bobbin. You would be surprised to see what happens to a medium blue top thread when you put a purple thread in the bobbin. We are so used to matching these threads, but with my freestyle quilting, that is no longer necessary. No way I am spending my time on hiding each and every thread in the back for a wall hanging! It seems silly to do this.

Batting and Quilt Sandwiches

Choose if you are putting your work directly on batting or if you will use a piece of fabric first for extra stability. I have done both, and I think it is best to put another fabric in between your work and the batting if you are planning on quilting intensely. If you do quilt intensely, foundation paper alone might not be sturdy enough. On the other hand, if you plan on quilting very little or not at all, extra fabric support is not needed. You can put your work straight on batting or a flannel.

In my quilt "Gene Pool," I used 82 threads for the top and 12 for the bobbin, showing how much thread might be needed.

This quilt layered batting directly on Pattern Ease before quilting.

Your quilt sandwich could also be collage, foundation, and batting, which are the typical layers in a quilt. When using an extra layer of fabric, fuse one-sided batting to the wrong side of the in-between fabric. Pin the collage on top of the fabric. The quilt sandwich becomes collage, foundation, support fabric, and batting. There is nothing against the bottom side of the batting yet. All that is lacking is backing fabric.

Some people like to mount their collage on canvas and will not use any batting at all. Their sandwich has only the collage and foundation.

Thread Options

For quilting, in general, 40 or 50 wt. thread will be your first choice, but any other weight will be fine as well. Color is more important than thread weight. If you want to make a Leader stand out, use a heavier thread (this is a thread with a lower number). On the other hand, very thin threads that will hardly be visible are great for Followers. This is an intense and precise job because, just like your fabrics, the thread colors need to follow the path. On a lighter color fabric, you want to use a lighter color thread. Yes, the threads will need to be changed often. My quilts have a lot of different color threads, but this helps with blending the colors.

It is not only the top thread, but the bottom-thread color is adjusted as well. If I don't have a perfect color for the top, using a different color in my bobbin can give the right adjustment. It is a matter of playing and trying things out.

I do understand not everyone has as many threads as I have been collecting over the years. You can limit the number of color changes, use a variegated thread, or use a monofilament thread, which takes a lot of the color hassle away. Thread is such a personal choice.

Quilting

I use a tiny free motion zigzag stitch on my Janome sewing machine. Unfortunately, not every machine has this stitch, which is only available on the higher-end machines. If you don't have a free motion zigzag stitch, you can use a regular free motion stitch. An allover free motion stitch with threads that match areas of the same color gives a lovely result. This is how I did it before I discovered the free motion zigzag stitch on my machine.

Even a straight or wonky quilt line with monofilament can work. It all depends how much you want to do and feel comfortable with. In general, though, the better you match the color of the thread, the less visible the quilting becomes. That's the effect I am looking for. The whole collage is about color, and the more I can bring out that color flow, the better.

Use any thread that matches the piece of fabric to sew it down.

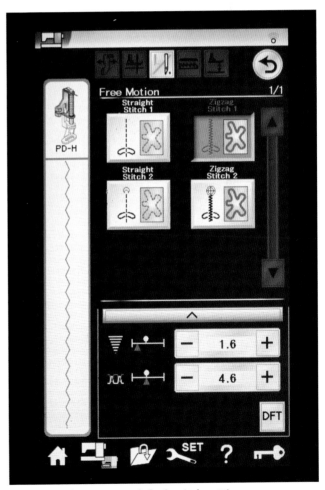

These have become my default stitch settings on my sewing machine.

You can stitch over the original color if the thread doesn't blend like you intended.

On my Janome, I bring the free motion zigzag stitch down to 1.6, which is very narrow. You can hardly see that it is a zigzag. It is more like an irregular straight stitch. With a thread matching the piece I want to stitch down, I move my needle about three stitches forward, then three stitches back, and then six forward. Three back, six forward. This way every piece will get stitched three times with an irregular stitch. This results in a look that is somewhere between thread painting and embroidery, a casual, organic way of attaching everything down.

I follow the shape of my fabrics. I think this style of quilting matches collage: it is not super regular on purpose, but at the same time, it frames the pieces of fabric. Nothing will fray, as there is no room for fraying. If you are ever not pleased with the color result, you can go over it again with another color. Very forgiving!

Starting in the middle of the quilt, stitch each and every piece down to the batting by following its shape. This is a big advantage—you don't have to come up

with a quilting pattern. The quilting follows what is already there.

This sewing down of all the pieces is a lot of work. It may take even longer than the collage itself. I enjoy this process, and it is very rewarding to see the blending of the colors happening in front of your eyes.

Backing

After all your stitching is done, press your quilt flat with a warm iron. You don't need to use a hot steam iron. This last phase is all about making the fibers relax and lay nicely flat. The large number of threads created a little bit of a mess on the other side of the batting. That's the reason there is no backing fabric yet. I wouldn't want to clean up all those thread beginnings and endings for a wall hanging. Also, I prefer to use some kind of stiffener to make sure the quilt is hanging nice and flat.

Look for backing and a piece of fusible stabilizer in the same size as the backing. The stabilizer is

The stabilizer is ironed onto the wrong side of the blue backing fabric, which is the final layer of the quilt sandwich.

getting fused to the wrong side of the backing, then these two connected layers go against the wrong side of the batting (the messy side). You can also use adhesive spray to fuse them. If you use Odif 505, use it moderately. It only has to hold the layers together until the stitching is done. Mistyfuse can also work. Put some patches on the back of your batting, and iron the entire top on the stabilizer.

As mentioned, I recommend using a "false back" for freestyle color collage. The problem is that some quilt shows will not accept false backings. For art shows, this is not an issue at all. If I want to enter into a quilt show, I will have to somehow show quilt stitches on the back,

but there is no rule about how many stitches have to be visible. The way to deal with this is to quilt in just a few places with the same zigzag stitch at the very end. It's "pretend quilting," and I don't mind finishing some threads nicely if that makes the quilt qualified for show entrance. Therefore, when I do the quilting, I skip the largest shapes and only do those when the backing is in place. Your quilt is ready for binding.

If you have decided to hardly quilt at all, give the quilt a straight stitch line ¼" (6.4mm) away from the edge, securing all layers. The stitch line will become invisible when the binding is attached. After that, you can trim the quilt.

Binding

A big thank you to Susan Carlson; I love using her "wrap-and-glue" technique for the binding. You could do a regular binding, but I think a binding that doesn't frame the work is much more appropriate. In regular quilting, you could face a quilt, but that is different in a collage quilt, especially if you have many small pieces near the edges. Facing would put too much stress on those little pieces.

The wrap-and-glue method is beautiful! It will give the collage an "open" end, which is the more artful solution these days. It looks as if the collage is continuing in the binding. That means two things: you are looking for fabrics in the colors of the edge, and you will have to cut these fabrics with that same curvy feel as you did the entire collage.

If you do this well, maybe you too will get the question someone asked me: "How are you going to do the binding?" The binding blended so well in with the edge of the quilt, this person couldn't see the binding!

Heads Up

As Susan herself warns, some judges at quilt shows will not like a glued binding. They prefer a regular binding. This happened to me with "Abundance," where the judge said it "would be better" to sew a regular binding. I respectfully disagree, but a judge has the last word at a quilt show. It could be a point of consideration for some.

1. Look for fabrics that match the edge colors. You may even have a same scrap left. Start on a corner by cutting a 3" x 3" (7.6 x 7.6cm) piece in the same color of the corner edge. Put this on the corner and double check to make sure it is big enough to cover both sides.

2. Cut a random corner piece off with scissors. This is the same style of curved cutting you did all during the collage. Put it back on the corner, and arrange for about ½" (1.3cm) of the quilt to be covered and about ¾" (1.9cm) of the piece to be sticking out on each end. These exact measurements are not so important.

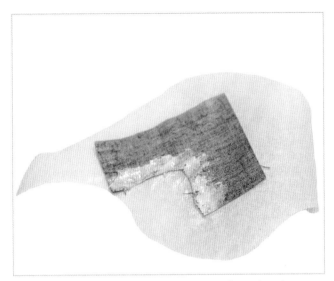

3. Flip the fabric wrong side up. Apply tacky glue to the curved side of the piece. Put a clean piece of paper underneath and smear the glue with your fingers, making sure the glue is completely covering the fabric for about ½" (1.3cm).

4. Put the glued corner piece on your corner. Press down. You don't have to be concerned about any glue somewhere else, as it dries invisible. However, you can leave the paper underneath if desired.

5. Fold one side over. Start at the spot furthest away from the corner. You can easily feel with your fingers how to make the fold. Don't stretch, just fold over. When you come to the corner, bring the fabric in a tiny bit more.

6. Put glue on the other side of the binding. Fold that piece over as well. The corner will come out perfectly.

7. Continue down the side. Use a new piece of fabric that matches that area of the quilt. In this example, I found a scrap of the same fabric as used in the collage, so placed it nearby. Cut about 1½" x 3" (3.8 x 7.6cm).

8. Cut one of the long sides with some curves. Flip to the wrong side up. Put a piece of paper underneath, and smear some tacky glue on the curved long side with your finger.

9. Apply the fabric about ½" (1.3cm) on the edge. Only the glued part is on the quilt, while the rest is sticking out. If possible, overlap a little bit of the matching fabric with the new scrap. Press well in place.

10. Flip the quilt, backing side facing up. Put a clean piece of paper underneath. Spread glue on the rest of the binding fabric and fold it over. You can feel the edge with your fingers. Make a smooth line without pulling it too tight, which is just a matter of folding over carefully. Finger press.

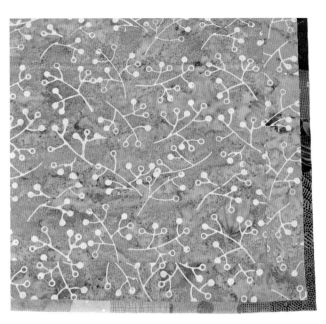

11. Look for the next piece of binding and repeat.
Each new piece should slightly overlap the previous one. All pieces should be 2"–3½" (5.1–8.9cm) in length, matching the nearest area of the collage.

12. Fix irregularities on the backing if desired.
Option one: trim all the pieces more or less to the same size before you glue them down. Option two: put another small strip of backing on top of the back binding and give it a more finished look. I do this when my quilts are selected for a show.

Once you get the hang of it, this technique is really just wrapping pieces of fabric on the quilt edges. Super simple and with a great result!

Students at Work

As much as I love creating freestyle color collages and seeing them displayed in quilt and art shows around the country, what truly gives me joy is teaching this technique to others. The best part is witnessing that "aha" moment when a line or pathway takes their work in an unexpected direction that's even better than they had envisioned. Use these works as inspiration as you continue your collage journey.

Student Kim Perez gets started on her first collage. You see some excellent large Leaders that set Kim up for her collage. Also see how she changed her mind and put fabrics elsewhere later. Kim's work has large areas in the same color that are slowly transitioning into another section. After hours of work, a beautiful color story is revealing itself!

Works in progress on an open studio day. As seen in the scraps, decision making happens all throughout the process.

Student Denise Cline has a big blue Leader that is making its way to the big yellow flower. She has found two excellent Connectors with blue and yellow. The more blue one is in the right spot. From the yellow Leader, she is making her way to the orange. Again, all Followers and Connectors are placed correctly, creating beautiful pathways. The pink paisley Leader has the same color light blue as the light blue Follower. She is picking that color up for a new line.

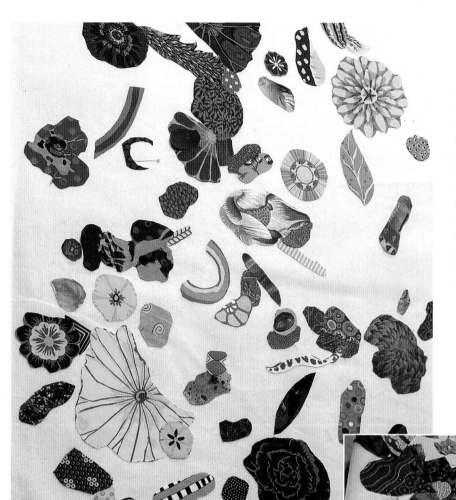

Already at the beginning, Deborah Child had great Leaders and Connectors. She was looking for a connection from that big green leaf to the dark purple flowers. In her search, she almost immediately discovered that black could help out. Deborah has a great eye for color because she divided the different oranges, greens, and purples well. All these sections will build out, but the lines are starting to show.

Student Cookie Shuffleton's collage in a color scheme of green, orange, and brown. She loves a busy design and uses a lot of Leaders and not as many Followers. It's a rich range of colors. Despite having many orange Leaders, she spaced them apart and transitions to them throughout the piece.

The beginning of a collage by student Marsha Webb, followed by Marsha's progress hours later. Look at how she started and ended. Fabrics have been moved around a lot. Great! She started with the green Leader in the middle right of the pink leaf Leader, but that ended up left. Purple was not on her mind when she started, but the color moved its way in.

I love her red line. It moves so well. I also love how she divided the more teal greens and bright greens. By putting it on opposite corners, the work has balance. It also turns the red into a warm stream.

About Carly

Carly Mul, a Dutch lawyer by education, discovered a passion for fabric when she was in her thirties and had moved with her family from The Netherlands to the United States in 1994. She took her first quilt classes in Roswell, Georgia, in 1995. From there, she started Box Emotions, a craft business in which she sold hundreds of fabric-covered handmade boxes all over the country.

In 2003, she founded Webfabrics. This business started in the basement of her home and grew into one of the largest and most successful quilt retailers on the East Coast of the US. Fabrics have been sold online, in the brick-and-mortar store in Purcellville, Virginia, and at most major quilt shows with a large presentation.

Carly's eye for color is well-known in the quilting world. Customers have used her knowledge for their projects, and as a store owner, she wrote a weekly newsletter in which she often described why a certain fabric was worth taking a closer look at. Carly gives lectures and workshops about trends in color and collage, her favorite style of quilting. She has been consulted by fabric companies for her input on collections. Carly has a broad knowledge of the quilting industry, the business side as well as the creative side.

Carly and her husband, Jan, are the proud parents of three children and their partners. They became grandparents for the first time in 2018 and now have four little granddaughters. The birth of her first granddaughter was a point in her life when Carly realized that running a successful business was consuming all her attention and that she wanted more. It was time to rebalance and find more time to be involved with the little ones, having time to travel, be involved in giving back to the community, and quilt herself.

After careful consideration, Carly sold Webfabrics in June 2022. She started to focus on her collage art and is excited that many works have been accepted at art and quilt shows, including International Quilt Festival Houston (2024). Her activities can be followed on her website www.carlymul.com.

She teaches at guilds as well as domestic and international shows; from time to time, she hosts Open Studio Days in her home for small groups of students. At her website www.collagefabric.com, she offers fabrics and supplies collage students and other quilters may need, especially super-small amounts of fabrics.

Together with her husband, Carly loves to travel around the world or within the US in their RV. They both love their role as grandparents and enjoy every minute with the little girls. Carly is a volunteer at the local food bank, plays competitive tennis, and loves gardening, especially growing vegetables and flowers.

Acknowledgments

A big thank-you needs to go toward all my customers during 19 years of owning a quilt store. They motivated me with their questions and comments. I could write a book about the wonderful memories they have given me.

Thank you to the students in my collage classes, who were eager to learn more about color and who were the ones asking me for a book explaining this way of making a collage.

A big thank-you also to all the designers and fabric companies for making fabric collections that continue to excite quilters. You are the driving force behind the art of quilting.

A special thank-you to my husband, Jan. Not only do I have his nonstop love and support, but he's also the photographer of my quilts, the administrator of my files, and the first editor of my writing.

Last but not least, I want to thank Fox Chapel for making this book a reality. It takes a big team of people, but I especially want to express my gratitude for Amelia Johanson, Senior Acquisitions Editor. Her input and enthusiasm were essential.

Index